Henry Lee

Lee's Guide to Saratoga, the Queen of Spas

Henry Lee

Lee's Guide to Saratoga, the Queen of Spas

ISBN/EAN: 9783337323479

Printed in Europe, USA, Canada, Australia, Japan

Cover: Foto ©Lupo / pixelio.de

More available books at **www.hansebooks.com**

GUIDE to SARATOGA

the QUEEN'S SPAS

HATHORN SPRING

GEYSER SPRING

CONGRESS HALL

CONGRESS PARK

PRICE 25 CENTS

LEE'S GUIDE

TO

SARATOGA,

THE

QUEEN OF SPAS.

CONTENTS :

*History and Analysis of the Springs, How to get there,
General Notes, Hotels, Boarding Houses, Amuse-
ments, Walks, Drives, Excursions, Races,
Churches, Medical & Public Institutions,
Commercial Features, and Condensed
History of Saratoga, &c.*

ILLUSTRATED WITH MAPS, WOOD CUTS,

AND A

PICTORIAL VIEW OF THE VILLAGE.

Spencer Trask & Co.,

BANKERS,

Nos. 16 & 18 Broad Street,

NEW YORK CITY.

Transact a General Banking Business

All Classes of Securities Bought and Sold on Commission, and Carried on Margins.

INTEREST ALLOWED ON DAILY BALANCES.

DEPOSITS RECEIVED SUBJECT TO SIGHT CHECKS,

OFFICES:

ALL CONNECTED BY PRIVATE WIRE.

PHILADELPHIA :
132 South Third Street.

BOSTON :
20 Congress Stree
63 Federal Street

ALBANY, N. Y.:
State Street cor. James.

PROVIDENCE, R. I.:
13 Westminster Street.

SARATOGA :
Grand Union Hotel.

WORCESTER :
415 Main Street.

GENERAL INDEX.

Pellucid Clearness of Skin and Complexion.

ARSENIC
Complexion Wafers,

A New and SAFE Form of Dispensing this Potent Remedy.

☞It is really Much Safer to take ARSENIC Internally Knowingly, with a "Perfect Accuracy" of Dose, than to Swallow it Unwittingly at hap hazard, Disguised as a "Mixture," or Patent Medicine.

Arsenic Complexion Wafers,

The ONLY REAL beautifier of the complexion, skin and form.

Face Lotions, Powder, Enamel and "Blood Purifiers," (so called) are a **delusion** *and a* **Snare.**

These Wafers are specially compounded by an experienced physician and chemist. Perfectly safe and harmless if used as directed, and magical in effects. 50 cts. and $1 per box.; sent by mail to any address; sample package, 25c. silver. To be had only by addressing

"ENGLISH CHEMIST,"
146 West 16th St., N. Y.

Elegant Contour of Form and Figure.

CHAPTER I

HOW TO REACH SARATOGA.

Saratoga Springs lies between the Hudson and Mohawk rivers, and is the largest village, al though not the county seat, of Saratoga county. Its population at the last census was 10,820, but its visitors number annually probably 60,000. Hence the various routes by which tourists may reach this Queen of Spas, is of the first import- ance. We will endeavor to place this before our readers in as plain, yet as concise a manner as possible. In two cases we shall give a description of the routes, viz: from the city of New York and from the city of Boston. In other cases we shall merely give the routes, line of railroad and where connections may, and in some cases must be made. To give the reader a general idea where Saratoga is, must be our first point.

It is near the eastern edge of New York, State and lies north from New York city 183 miles, from Boston west 230 miles, from Niagara Falls, south-east 312 miles, from Montreal due south 200 miles, from Philadelphia 274 miles Washington 412, and from Chicago, via Niagara Falls, 841 miles.

The routes by both rail and boat are numerous

but they finally resolve themselves into two railroads; one the Delaware & Hudson Canal Co's railroad which runs through the town, and the other the Boston, Hoosac Tunnel & Western, which has its terminus on Lake Avenue in Saratoga. Our first route will be from

NEW YORK TO SARATOGA.

There is scarcely any doubt but that two-thirds of the visitors to this far famed watering place come from, or by way of New York. It is therefore of the first importance, that the visitor should have the various routes fairly placed before him, so that a choice may be made to suit his time or inclinations. Probably the first in order is the

NEW YORK CENTRAL & HUDSON RIVER RAILROAD,

Probably this line has done more to popularize Saratoga with New Yorkers, than all the other modes of transit combined, and certainly carry more passengers than are carried on all the other routes. The Grand Central Depot in New York can be reached from any part of the city, by either surface or elevated roads. The two favorite trains during the season which run through without change, are those leaving at 9 a. m. and 3.30 p. m., arriving in Saratoga at 2.00

and 8.30 p. m. respectively. They are both special
Saratoga trains, and have been run by this Company
for the last 16 years; other trains leave at 11 a.
m., 6.30 and 11 p. m.; time of journey is about
$5\frac{1}{2}$ hours, and the fare $4.20. The best trains for
returning are those leaving Saratoga at 8.40 a. m.,
1 p. m. and 4 p. m., arriving at the Grand Central
Depot, New York, at 2.12, 7 and 9.20 p. m. respectively. The Saratoga office of this line during the season, is at the corner of Broadway and
Spring Street, where tickets for all points, also
Drawing Room and Sleeping Car accommodation,
can be obtained.

Taking the river route, probably the first in
order is the

DAY LINE OF STEAMERS.

The boats of this line leave (pier 39) North
River, foot of Vestry streer, New York, daily,
except Sunday at 8.30 a. m., and pier foot of
Twenty-second street, North River, at 9 a. m.
These boats make several landings going up the
river and arrive in Albany about 6 p. m., where
connection is made with evening trains for Saratoga and the North.

Continuing our river route the next in order
is the

Hudson River by Daylight.

THE FAVORITE DAY LINE STEAMERS,

"ALBANY," "C.VIBBARD" OR "DANIEL DREW"

Daily (except Sundays) leave

NEW YORK—Vestry St. Pier 8.40, and West 22d St. 9 A. M.

For ALBANY, landing at Nyack and Tarrytown, (by ferry,) West Point, Newburg, Poughkeepsie, Rhinebeck, Catskill, and Hudson.

Returning leave Albany at 8:30 a. m. Close connection made at Albany to and from SARATOGA by Special Express train, arriving in Saratoga at 8 p. m., and leaving 7 a. m.

Tickets Sold and Baggage Checked through over all connecting roads,

THE HUDSON RIVER.

The Hudson river is too famous among the rivers of the world to require its geographical position to be given. All the world knows that the great city of New York lies at its mouth; that it flows nearly south along the eastern counties of the State of New York; that it has its source in the Adirondack Mountains, three hundred miles from its mouth, and four thousand feet above the level of the sea.

The best way to see the Hudson is from the deck of one of these fine steamboats that daily ascend and descend its current. Let the traveler get a position if possible on the forward-deck, inasmuch as the scene is far more striking and effective when both shores can be taken in at once; while the traveler thus placed has the opportunity of enjoying a succession of surprises that, amid the Highlands specially, give zest to the picture.

Leaving New York, the New Jersey shore forms the western bank. The first place to pass is Hoboken, famous for its German beer gardens, then come the Weehawken hills, after passing Spuyten Duyvil and Manhattanville, we come to Fort Washington on the east, and Fort Lee on the west bank. After Fort Lee come the Palisades. For a distance of twenty miles, on the western shore.

On the eastern shore however, is a different picture; first we come to Riverdale, then two miles further north to Yonkers, then Hastings, where Washington had his head-quarters in 1783, and twenty-four miles from New York, Irvington, on the opposite side the monotonous palisades having disappeared we come to Nyack, a very picturesque town, opposite to which is Tarrytown.

In its craft, the Hudson has attractions much greater than those of other rivers. The Rhine is vacant and dull in this particular. Our Western rivers have little more than steamboats and a few rafts. On the Hudson there are grand steamboats, brilliant, ³ bird-like yachts, great, broad-sailed sloops, groups of square barges, and vast fleets of canal-boats in tow; the variety and the number are so great that the scene is at all times animated by them, and reminds one of the Mersey at Liverpool, or the Thames near London.

We now come to Sing Sing, famous for its prison, and four miles further to Croton, from whose lake New York city receives its supply of fresh water, and next comes the town of Peekskill.

We now enter the Highlands, which, from this point to Newburg, a distance of seventeen miles, is unsurpassed by any river-scenery in the world. To our left is Dunderberg, or Thunder Mountain, whose steep sides are perpetually in

voking gusts of wind and rain on its rugged and
and bold crest.

Near this point is a picturesque island, called
Iona, of some three hundred acres in extent,
lying within a triangle formed by Dunderberg,
Anthony's Nose, and Bear Mountain. Grapes
are grown extensively upon the island, and the un-
cultivated portion is a favorite picnic-ground for
excursion-parties from New York.

Next we come to West Point (fifty-one miles
from New York), the world-known great Military
Academy.

Opposite to West Point, on the eastern bank,
is the active village of Cold Spring, which is fifty-
four miles from New York.

Night in the Highlands, indeed, is scarcely less
lovely than the day. The river breaks with the
faintest murmur on the precipitous shore; the
walls of the mountains are an impenetrable black-
ness, against which the starry path overhead
looks the more lustrous. Trembling echoes strike
the hill-sides plaintively, as a great steamer
cleaves her way up the stream, or a tow-boat,
with a string of canal-boats in her wake, strug-
gles against the tide; while fleets of sailing-ves-
sels drift past.

The steamer now turns a little to the west, and
runs toward Cornwall landing, which is fifty-six
miles from New York. Cornwall is a charming

town, crowded with cottages and summer boarding-houses.

Fishkill Landing is sixty miles from New York. The Mattewan Creek here empties into the Hudson. The Dutchess & Columbia Railway terminates here.

Newburgh.—Opposite from Fishkill Landing and upon the declivity of a hill, is Newburgh. It has a population of eighteen thousand. During the revolution, Newburgh was for some time the encampment of the American army, and there it was disbanded, June 23, 1783.

Poughkeepsie, seventy-five miles from New York, has a population of twenty-two thousand. It derives its name from the Indian word *Apo-keep-sing,* which signifies "safe harbor." The city is built partly on the hillside, but chiefly on an elevated plateau, in the rear of which is College Hill, five hundred feet above tide water.

Next is Rhinebeck, with Rondout across the river, and one hundred and eleven miles from New York we reach Catskill, with its mountains, hotels, and falls. Six miles further to the town of Hudson, passing Athens, Coxsackie, Kinderhook and Castleton, we reach the wharve at the city of Albany.

Before Albany was incorporated, it was variously known as Beverwyck, Williamstadt, and New Orange. Its growth was exceedingly slow, and a hundred years from its incorporation could only boast of a population of ten thousand. But when Fulton succeeded in his experiments, and the steam-navigation of the Hudson became an accomplished fact, and when the Erie Canal was completed, and discharged immense loads of produce in the great basin, which is now the harbor of hundreds of boats, Albany attracted an increase of more than fifty thousand to its population in less than fifty years. Two hundred years ago it was surrounded by wooden walls, with loop-holes for musketry, and six gates, the ruins of which were in existence until 1812; but now, with a population of nearly seventy thousand, it is laid out with handsome avenues and drives, and will soon possess one of the most magnificent legislative buildings in the world.

Eight railways terminate in, or pass through it; its manufactories consist principally of stove-foundries and breweries ; its sales of barley amount to over two million bushels a year, and its trade in lumber and cattle is equally large. The public buildings, besides the Capitol, include the celebrated Dudley Observatory, the State Arsenal, the State Library, and the University. On the flats above the city is the Schuyler House, the home of the first mayor of Albany, and in the northern part is the Van Rensselaer Manor, the home of the first patroon—two of the most interesting historic houses in America.

We leave Albany by the Delaware and Hudson
Canal Co's Railroad, whose trains run to and
from the steamboat landings, and whose depot
adjoins that of the N. Y. C & H. R. R., so that
there is no need to fear missing connection, nor
any trouble in the transfer of baggage.

Six miles above Albany is Troy, a city with a
population of nearly fifty thousand. It is an active thriving city, with many large manufactories,
handsome churches, and elegant private residences.

Next is *Waterford* then *Cohoes*, sometimes
called the "City of Spindles." An immense
water-power is here formed by the Mohawk River,
which makes a descent of a hundred feet. The
Cohoes Falls, about a half-mile above the railroad
bridge, have a perpendicular descent of forty
feet. Here are situated numerous knitting and
cotton mills, axe and edge-tool factories, which
give a commercial importance to the city, and
employment to thousands of operatives.

Mechanicville, thirteen miles from Troy, is a
smart manufacturing town. A monument erected
to the memory of Col. Ellsworth, of the famous
Ellsworth Zouaves, will be found in the quiet
cemetry on the hill.

Passing Round Lake noted for its camp-meet-
ings we come to

which is twenty-six miles from Troy, and the county-seat of Saratoga County. The Kayaderosseras Creek, which flows through the village, furnishes a fine water-power for the numerous paper-mills, emery-wheel works, sash and box factories, &c., situated along its banks.

The village has a population of about three thousand people ; has many fine buildings, both public and private, and is supplied with pure water, and good schools, which render it a desirable location for a permanent home.

Ballston Spa derives its celebrity from the mineral springs which flow here in great abundance.

The artesian springs flow from a depth of six hundred feet through solid rock. The Sans Souci Hotel was built many years ago by Nicholas Low, and in its plan and surroundings does much credit to the taste and liberality of the proprietor. It is 160 feet long, with two wings extending back 153 feet, and is calculated for the accommodation of one hundred and fifty boarders. The Sans Souci Spring, which is within the grounds of the hotel, is seven hundred feet deep.

At Ballston an agent of the Saratoga Baggage Express generally joins the train, and in the seven miles run before arriving at Saratoga he goes through the train, soliciting baggage checks.

This company is recognized as a responsible con-
cern and visitors need have no fear but that their
baggage will be safely delivered at their hotel or
boarding-house within a very short time of their
arrival. Their charges are also reasonable, being
only twenty-five cents.

BOSTON TO SARATOGA.

The visitor in coming from, or by way of
Boston, must come by rail, unless he prefers the
round-about way of going to New York, and
then taking the river boats, but presuming he
will take the shortest route, then he will come by
the Boston, Hoosac Tunnel and Western Railway, This company since last year have acquired
what was the Saratoga Lake Railway and have
now a separate entrance and terminus on Lake
avenue in Saratoga Springs. Few, if any, roads
are richer in objects of interest and beauty of
scenery along their routes than the Boston,
Hoosac Tunnel and Western. The road extends
through a country deversified by mountains and
valleys, blooming with well tilled farms, smiling
with meadows and pastures with all their delightful accompaniment of wild flowers, and sugges-
tions of rural life, romantic in scenes of rugged
cliffs, deep gorges and spots of traditional renown
and rich in the variety of bustling towns, busy
villages and cosy, quiet hamlets. Almost along

the entire route the Hoosac river pushes itself into notice ; now flowing quietly along by the side of the track, now rushing noisily over a stony bottom, now tumbling to pieces over the jagged edge of some minature precipice, now shining in an open meadow and now peeping, cool and dark, between narrow banks and overhanging trees, and disappearing from the gaze by a sudden turn in the road, and as suddenly appearing again, all the while keeping company with the traveller, and refreshing one by its presence, until the lordly Hudson comes in view and the magnificient scene at Mechanicville is spread before the sight.

In giving a description of the prominent effects along the route, mention must be made of that monument of faith and triumph of engineering skill, the *Hoosac Tunnel*. This tunnel took years upon years to make and the mishaps and disasters were neither "few nor far between," difficulties of every nature were met with, seemingly insurmountable at times ; bit by bit, the rock and dirt were removed, until the tunnel was an established fact and to-day thousands can relate the novel experience of riding miles through the heart of a great mountain in perfect safety. The tunnel cost literally a "mint o' money" and the sacrifice at various periods, of nearly 200 lives.

Arriving at *North Adams* we find a thriving
manufacturing town growing with almost Western
rapidity. It has been named "The Tunnel City"
and is widely known for its enterprise and the
sociability of its people, its lovely natural surroundings, its fine hotels, elegant church edifices
and admirable schools. The population is about
12,000. Leaving the handsome union depot, we
roll through the "little tunnel" past the
"gingham ground" on the right, the village
cemetery on the left, the grounds of the agricul-
tural society, again to the right, and then on we
speed by *Bragtonville*, to *Blackinton*, a pretty
little village of 1,000 inhabitants. We next
come to *Williamstown*, quite a model village, a
well known summer resort and the seat of Wil-
liams' College.

Passing *Pownal* a farming section where the
crops are raised on the sides of the hills, we come
to *North Pownal*, a very pretty place and on to
Petersburgh Junction, where a connection is
made with the Harlem extension to Bennington and
other points north. Two or three miles further on
we come to *Hoosac* quite a romantic looking village
and then on to *Hoosac Falls*. This is by far the
most important way station on the route, and is
making very rapid progress. The population at
present being from 5,000 to 6,000. The curve at
this point over a high-made bank gives a fine

view of the falls. *Hathaway*, is a flag station from which we run to *Eagle Bridge*. At this point a junction is made with the Delaware and Hudson, Rutland and Washington branch, then to *Bieskieks*, a farming village and to *Johnsonville*, quite a manufacturing centre, then to *Valley Falls*, with its cotton, grist and saw mills and about nine miles from Mechanicville is *Schaghticoke* a place of great natural beauty and historical interest. The valley which lies at the junction of Tomhannock creek with the Hoosac is nearly circular, and contains about 1200 acres. The entire valley is full of romance, and traditional stories of border warfare, almost every farm having its legend of pioneer life or warlike incident. We next come to *Mechanicville*, a very important junction and until the acquisition of the Saratoga Lake Railway the western terminus of the line. The engine houses of B. H. T. & W. R'y are located here. Just before the train draws up at the station we cross the Hudson river over a double track, iron bridge 2000 feet long, affording a view up and down this mighty river and of the level country for miles around,* connection is here made with the Delaware and Hudson line. The population is over 3000, and is rapidly increasing, new mills have recently been erected here for the manufacture of wood pulp into paper. The buildings, machinery &c., are said to have cost over half a million dollars. At Mechanicville an agent of the Saratoga Baggage Express will join the train to collect checks and arrange for the delivery of visitors baggage. Leaving *Mechanicville* we come upon historic ground, viz : Saratoga's battle ground, a station being very aptly named *Battle Ground Station*, from which stages can be taken to Stillwater, Schuylerville and Bemis Heights. Coming along we come to Ketchums Corners for White Sulpher Springs and hotel. *Cedar Bluff* is the next station at which is a fine hotel on the edge of Saratoga Lake, it is the property of the same company, as is also further on the Fonda House, at the north end of the Lake. A large steamer Lady of the Lake connects with different points of interest on the Lake. Then on to Eureka Spring, Excelsior Spring, passing the Loughberry Water works, the "A," Red, Empire, Star, High Rock, Seltzer and Magnetic Springs, we run into the station at Saratoga, and within five minntes walk of all the principal hotels.

Another route from Boston is by the Boston and Albany R. R. to Springfield, Mass., and Albany, N. Y., thence via Saratoga Division of the Delaware and Hudson Canal Co.'s R. R. to Saratoga. Passengers by this route can if they prefer,diverge at south Framingham, via Boston, Clinton, Fitchburg and New Bedford R. R., to Fitchburg, Mass. Distance, via Hoosac Tunnel route, 231 miles, via Cheshire R. R., 238 miles. Palace cars are run from Boston to Saratoga without change via all these lines.

From *Maine* and the maritime provinces, rail or boat may be taken to Boston or to Portland. From Portland the Boston and Maine railroad connects with Manchester, N. H., and then, via Concord and Northern railroad, to White River Junction, Vt., thence, via Bellows Falls and Rutland, to Saratoga. Or from White River Junction take Central Vermont railroad to Burlington, Vt., thence, by steamer on Lake' Champlain or Central Vermont railroad, to Ticonderoga, N. Y., thence by Delaware and Hudson Canal Company's railroad to Saratoga ; or on from Burlington, via Central Vermont, to Rutland, and thence by Delaware and Hudson Canal Company's railroad to Saratoga. Or from Portland, Me., take Portland and Odgensburg railroad to White Mountains, St. Johnsbury, Vt., Cambridge and Burlington and thence by rail or steamer, as above.

From the *White Mountains* a through palace car is run to Saratoga in one day in summer, via the Wells river and Montpelier railroad, Central Vermont railroad, and Delaware and ↓ Hudson Canal Company's railroad, via Wells river, Montpelier, Burlington, Leicester Junction, Ticonderoga and Whitehall, to Saratoga.

Or by Portland and Ogdensburg railroad from White Mountains to Cambridge and Burlington, Vt., thence by rail or steamer.

From *Montreal* the most direct route is by the Delaware and Hudson Canal Company's line to Rouse's Point, and thence to Saratoga. Palace cars are run through from Montreal to Saratoga and New York.

Another route from Montreal is via the Grand Trunk railroad to St. John's, thence via Central Vermont to Rutland, where you change cars; thence, via Delaware and Hudson Canal Company's railroad, to Saratoga.

Or by Grand Trunk railroad to Rouse's Point, Lake Champlain steamers to Ticonderoga, and thence by *Delaware and Hudson Canal Company's railroad, to Saratoga Springs. The latter route is the more delightful, as it takes the tourist through the glorious scenery of Lake Champlain on the fine steamers of the lake, and also allows a divergence at Ticonderoga, via Lake George.

From *Philadelphia.*—To New York by the shortest route, and then by steamer or rail to Saratoga.

From *Baltimore.*—To New York, and then by steamer or rail to Saratoga.

From *Washington.*—To New York, and then by steamer or rail to Saratoga.

From the *Southeast.*—To New York, and then by steamer or rail to Saratoga.

From *Chicago.*—Via Buffalo, Niagara Falls and Albany to Saratoga.

From *Cincinnati.*—Via Buffalo and Albany to Saratoga.

From *San Francisco* and the *Far West.*—Via Chicago, Niagara Falls and Albany to Saratoga.

From *St. Louis.*—Via Indianapolis, Buffalo and Albany to Saratoga. By taking the Chicago route, the tourist can also visit Niagara Falls. Proceed thence via Albany.

From *New Orleans.*—By steamers on the Mississippi to St Louis, affording the tourist some delightful scenery. From St. Louis the most interesting route is by Chicago and Niagara Falls.

Or from New Orleans to Cincinnati, and thence, via Buffalo and Albany, to Saratoga.

From the *Southwest* and *Mexico.*—By rail to St. Louis, Chicago, Niagara Falls and Albany to Saratoga. Or by coastwise steamers to New York, and thence by rail or boat to Albany and Saratoga.

From *Europe.*—Tourists usually choose New York as the starting-place for Saratoga, as the route includes the Hudson river, giving a choice of boat or rail.

VIEW OF EXCELSIOR SPRING AND A PORTION OF EXCELSIOR PARK.
SARATOGA SPRINGS, N. Y.

CHAPTER II.

THE VILLAGE.

The *Pictorial Map* accompanying this guide is a perfect picture of the village, showing each house in its proper place and in its proportions. Each public building, church, hotel and spring has a number on its building in the map corresponding with the index.

The village of Saratoga, where dwells the benign.goddess Hygeia in the midst of her far-famed waters of life and health, is most pleasantly hidden within the heart of a broad stretch of varied table-land, in the upper part and near the eastern boundary of the great State of New York. The location is not remarkable for natural beauty, yet its immediate surroundings are by no means without attractions, while within easy reach, all about, may be found many of those beautiful landscape scenes for which the Empire State is so justly renowned.

The village, while most agreeably secluded from, is yet within the easiest and speediest reach of the busy world around. It is large enough to boast of a fixed population of some eleven thousand, which is trebled in summer-time by foreign incursion ; and it possesses in abundance all the

many ways and means of convenient and pleasurable life, in a liberal furniture of churches,
schools, stores, shops, and all other appointments
of home and social ease and comfort ; with all of
which it still retains a quiet country aspect.
Even the most thronged portions of the village,
where stand the great summer hotels, the flaming
emporiums of the city modes, and all the transient glare and glitter of congregated fashion, are
gratefully tempered by the screening and cooling
shade of verdant trees ; while reaching far around
this more busy region, stretch long avenues of
picturesque cottages, interspersed agreeably with
more stately villas and manorial homes.

In approaching Saratoga Springs over its various railways, the traveler meets with a surprise.
The change from open farms to close-built town
is abrupt, and the cars are among the houses and
at the station almost before the fields are missed.
From the south the first intimation is the little
group of cottages clustered about the Geyser
Springs, perhaps three minutes before the train
stops. From the north the new villas and
springs of Excelsior Park, the towers and mansard roofs of the great hotels, flash past just as
the brakes begin to pull up for the depot. The
long platforms swarm with importunate hackmen,
and were it not for good policing, the arrival
would be a trifle formidable. The prudent pas-

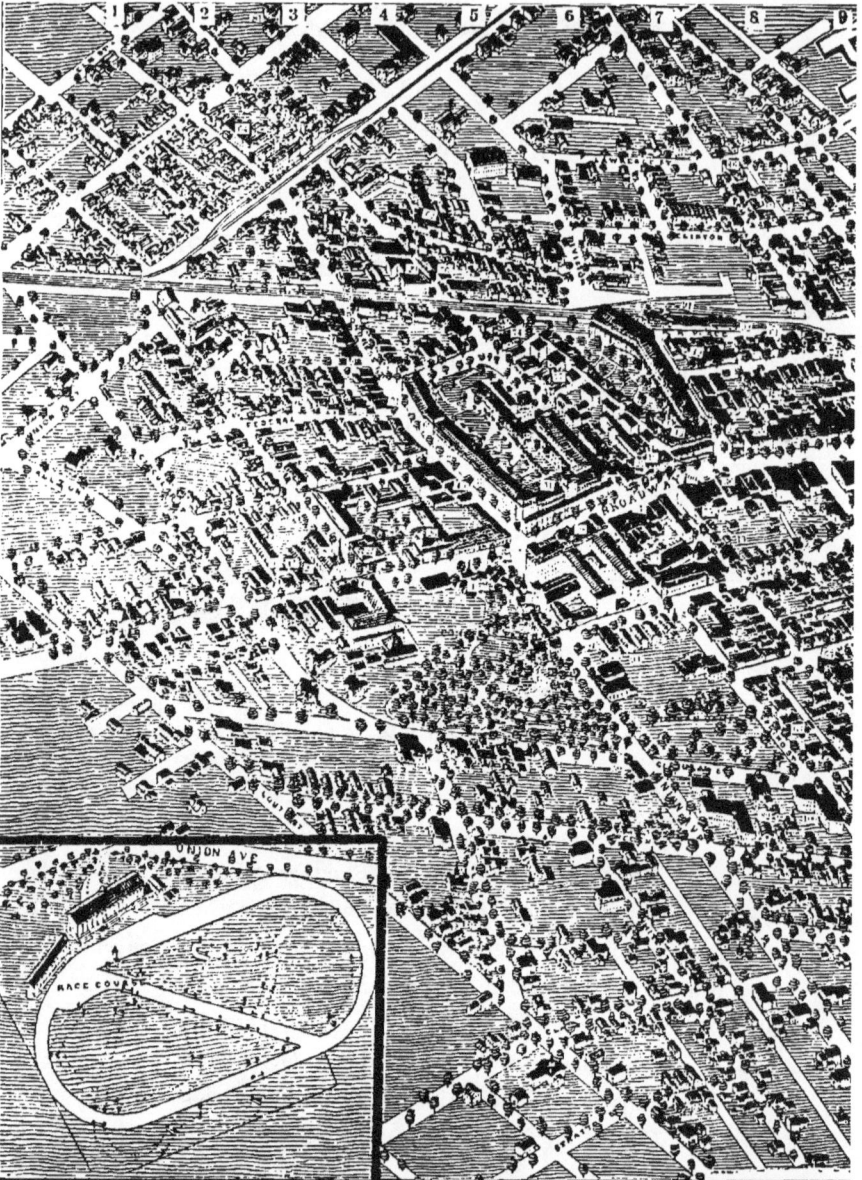

MEMORIAL VIEW OF SARATOGA

ned to the Index.—The first
se figure and letter, viz., 16 G.
the letters and figures around
lock or two of the place you de-
ond with the same in the Index.

er, P. D. . . . . 6 T
ill, R. . . . . 12 I
: St. House . . . 10 I
d Mhaabe . . . 9 F
E. . . . . 4 D
s, J. C. . . . . 8 G
d Hall . . . . 11 G
Housе . . . .
al Mayer . . . 11 F

CHURCHES.

61 Marston, M. A. . . . 7, 8 D
62 Morey, N. D. . . . 6 C
63 Morse, M. E. . . . 6 I
64 Pitney House . . . 3 D
65 Scovill, J. F. . . . 8 M
66 Smith, C. S. . . . 11 K
67 Terwilliger, S. . . . 1 G
68 Thorn, C. A. . . . 0 I
69 Vanderburgh, J. . . . 9 I
70 Vandercour, M. C. . 13 E
71 Walker, S. — . . . 16 D
72 Washington Hall . . 13 B
73 Wheeler . . . . .
74 Baptist Church . . . 6 E

75 Congregational . . . 7 G
76 M. E. Chapel . . . 6 K
77 M. E. Church . . . 6 K
78 Newland Church . . 5 K
79 Presbyterian . . . 10 F
80 Roman Catholic . . 5 G
81 Second Presbyterian . 7 A
82 P. M. Church . . . 1 J

PUBLIC INSTITUTES.
American U. Tel. Office . . 4 F
Citizen's Line Sth. Office . 6 F
Congress Park . . . 8, 6, 0 H
Day Line Sth. Office, N. Y. & Alb. 0 F
Dimue's College . . . 2 F
Dr. Strong's Institute . . 6 J

People's Line Sth. Office . 8 F
Post Office . . . 7 F
I. R. Depot . . . 6, 7 D
N. R. Express Office . . 7 D
Saratoga Club House . . 6 H
Saratoga Racing Association 6 H
Saratoga Daily and Weekly . 7 F
Saratoga Register . . . 8 F
Saratoga Sentinel . . . 8 F
Saratoga Sun . . . 8 F
Sisters of St. Joseph . . 4 J
Temple Grove Seminary . 0 F
Town Hall . . . 9, 10 F
Town Office . . . 9, 10 F
W. U. Tel. Office . . . 8 I

GRAND UNION HOTEL—Opposite Grand Central Depot, New York City.

Travelers, Tourists and Families arriving at Grand Central Depot to visit Saratoga, Niagara, White Mountains, Long Branch, or other Summer resorts, save $3.00 carriage hire by stopping at this hotel, and their baggage transferred to and from said depot to this House in ten minutes free of expense. **613** Rooms, fitted up at a cost of One Million Dollars—European Plan, **$1.00** per day and upwards. Elegant suites for families. Dining Room, Restaurant, Cafe, Lunch and Wine Rooms supplied with the best at moderate prices. **Families** can live better for less money at the **Grand Union** than at any other first-class hotel in the city.

W. D. GARRISON, Manager.

senger will provide for the transportation of his baggage, before he reaches the depot, by giving up his checks to the agent of the Saratoga Baggage Express.

To find the porter of your house, a glance at the row of signs overhead will show just where the correct man stands, and where you shall go to find him. Each hotel has a reliable man under its sign, and the badge on his hat will make the assurance sure.

Many of the larger hotels and houses meet every train with busses, and those who have not put you in a carriage, and in either case you are driven to your destination without charge. This is a village of vast hotels, and a party of six or more is a small affair where twenty thousand people may be lodged at once. Opposite the station rise the huge yellow walls of the United States Hotel, and the street beside it—Division street—leads one to the left, directly upon Broadway, the main thoroughfare of the village. Reaching this street, with the United States on the southern corner (right), and the Arlington Hotel on the northern corner (left), we find ourselves in the centre of the town. The street is supposed to run up to the north or left and down to the south or right. The United States, Grand Union, Congress Hall, Columbian, Clarendon and Everett are to the right ; the Arlington, Holden, Waverly and Broadway Hall are to the left, and each faces the street.

Saratoga is essentially American, and differs very materially from similar places on the European continent viz.: Harrogate, Bath and Cheltenham in England, Seltzer, Baden Baden and Aix of Germany, all noted for their mineral springs, where the wealth and fashion congregate. But there is more room in any of those places ; here, the beginning and the end is a few hundred yards on Broadway. There are few manufactories, and its streets are devoted to elegant leisure or abundant shopping. Its surface is mainly level, except where a shallow valley winds in a general northeasterly direction through the centre. Through this runs a little brook, and by its banks, at the bottom of the valley may be found some of the more famous mineral springs. The Town Hall, on the corner of Broadway and Lake avenue, marks the centre of population. The geographical centre is perhaps a quarter of a mile to the southeast of this point.

The principal street is Broadway,‘ extending through the entire village, and making the grand drive and promenade, where all the life, business and pleasure of the place may be seen in a five-minutes' walk. This concentration of the hotels and stores in one street, and in the immediate neighborhood of nearly all the springs, gives the village a singular aspect; for, away from this centre, there is nothing but houses, cottages and villas, each, in prim fashion, facing its quiet, shady street—a village of homes.

Broadway is original. The hotels, the stores, the fine rows of trees, the broad borders of sod, and the throng of carriages and people that crowd its walks and roads, present a spectacle unlike anything else in the world. Newport and Interlaken, Ems and Long Branch, have their special charms, but nowhere else is so much of caravansary and general splendor concentrated in so limited a space. No other resort can show three such palaces as the United States, to the north, and the Grand Union and Congress Hall, facing each other, on one street. There is too much of architectural glory; but the American likes grandeur, and here he has it in a profusion perfectly dazzling. The walks are good and the roads well kept. Thousands crowd the way in elegant attire, and there is a world of faces to see and admire. The throng of carriages pass in brilliant procession, flowers and elegant drapery fill the windows and frame the faces looking out, making a bit of realistic fairy-land that wins the attention at every step. The view of the village from the top of the large hotels or the Town Hall is very delightful. The numerous shade trees give the town the appearance of a beautiful forest

city, and the view will fully repay the slight
trouble of a few steps to one of these elevations.

Nor are sanitary essentials neglected. With
all the paint and varnish, sod-work and gilding,
there is no slighting of the unseen works upon
which the health and well-being of every town
must be built. Loughberry Lake furnishes abundant supplies of pure water, and, by the use of the
Holly system of waterworks, it is delivered at
every door for domestic and fire purposes.
Every street is lighted with gas, and the sewer-
age is abundantly provided for.

Saratoga has been so modest that its many advantages as a place of residence are often overlooked. That it possesses not a few unusual and
delightful attractions, while it is not behind
other places of its size in scarcely any respect,
must be acknowledged. Not alone the constant
use of its spring waters, but its dry and bracing
climate, its magnificent groves and finely shaded
streets—these and numerous other favorable cir-
cumstances contribute to make Saratoga unsurpassed as a permanent home. At one portion of
the year the most distinguished, cultivated and
wealthy of our country are gathered here, and
sight-seeing can be done at home and on our own
doorsteps. The many blessings which follow in
the train of wealth and culture are found here.
Travelers from other climes who visit our country

seldom return until they have drank from these celebrated fountains, and enjoyed the comforts of these mammoth hotels.

Notwithstanding all these benefits, which the resident population enjoy, the expense of living is moderate, and certainly below other and less celebrated watering-places. That these advantages are becoming appreciated is evinced by the numerous and costly dwellings that are being erected on almost every street.

Its elevation above tide-water is 306 feet, being 40 feet higher than Lake George. The population is about 11,000. Its streets are adorned with elegant buildings and shade-trees. Its hotels, in their size, keeping and decoration, are something wonderful. ' The springs are the most remarkable in the world. The waters have become an article of commerce, and all nations are its customers.

CHAPTER III.

HISTORY OF SARATOGA.

(Condensed from N. B. Sylvester's History of Saratoga Co.)

Around the name of Saratoga there clusters a wealth of historic lore. Since the name was first transferred from the oral language of the red man to the written page of the white man—in a word, from the favorite old hunting-ground of the river hills, first, to the little hamlet of the wilderness, and then to the town and county—it has been associated in peace as well as in war with the most important events which have been chronicled in our country's history. Within the territory now comprised in the county of Saratoga once lay the hunting-grounds of the Mohawk branch of the Iroquois or Five Nations. One of the most famous of these hunting-grounds was called by them Sa-ragh-to-ga, and from this the county derives its name.

It will thus be seen that, unlike New York, Boston or Albany, the name is purely American. The first time we find any mention of Saratoga is in 1684. It was not then the name of a town nor of a county, neither was it the name of a great summer resort; but it was the name of an old Indian hunting-ground, located along both sides

of the Hudson. This river, after breaking
through its last mountain barrier above Glen's
Falls, runs through a wide valley till it reaches
the bordering hills at a point nearly opposite to
Saratoga Lake. This old hunting-ground was
situated where the outlying hills begin to crowd
down to the river-banks, and was called, in the
significant Indian tongue, Se-rach-ta-gue, or the
" hillside country of the great river." It has
also been said that Saratoga, in the Indian language, means the "place of the swift water," in
allusion to the rapids and falls that break the
stillness of the stream, where the hillside country
begins on the river. An Indian, whose name was
O-ron-hia-tek-ha of the Caugh-na-wa-ga, and who
was well acquainted with the Mohawk dialect,
stated that Saratoga was from the Indian Sa-ra
ta-ke, meaning "a place where the track of the
heel may be seen."

Whether its meaning be this, that or the other,
it must be gratifying to all Americans that this
famous resort, situated as it is on American soil,
bears an American name. As early as 1684 this
hillside country, the ancient Se-rach-ta-gue, was
sold by the chiefs of the Mohawks to Peter
Philip Schuyler and six other citizens of Albany,
and the sale was confirmed by the English government. This old hunting-ground then became
known in history as the Saratoga patent, or on

some old maps as So-roe-to-gos-land. But it will be seen that the ground on which the village of Saratoga Springs is built, and the region in which the famous mineral springs are found, formed no part of the old hunting-ground or the Saratoga patent. The So-roe-to-gos-land of the olden time was fifteen miles in length and twelve miles in width, being six miles wide on either side of the river Hudson, and embraces amongst others at this time the townships of Saratoga and Stillwater.

The Indian name for the ground upon which Saratoga Springs is built was Kay-ad-ros-se-ra, and was the favorite hunting-ground of the Iroquois tribe. The forests were full of game, and its lakes and streams swarmed with fish. The sturgeon would sun itself in the basin below Gaha-oose, now Cohoes Falls, and the herring came up the Hudson river through Fish creek, giving rise to its name, and then into Lake Saratoga; and it is even said that whales in the good old times used to come up the Hudson as far as this hunting-ground. In fact, Vanderdonck says "that in the year 1647 two whales came up the river. One turned back, but the other was stranded not far from Cohoes Falls." The wild animals were probably the first discoverers of the Saratoga mineral springs, for they were attracted here in great numbers, so much so that

the Mohawks, the Iroquois, the Oneidas and On-
ondagas, and sometimes the farther-off Cayugas
and Senecas, built their hunting lodges in the
vicinity of the springs every summer. It will
thus be seen that wild, ancient Kayadrossera was
as famous in the olden time to the red man as
modern Saratoga is to-day to the white.

The tract of land known by the Indian name
of Kayadrossera, was purchased by Mr. Broughton and others from the Indians, and an Indian
deed given the 6th day of October, 1704 is signed
by the sachems of the tribe. On the 2nd day of
November, 1708, a patent was granted by Her
Majesty Queen Anne, to "her loving subjects
Nanning Hermance, Johannes Beekman, Rip Von
Dam," and ten others of the whole of Kayadros-
era, but it was not until the year 1768 that the
deed given by the Indians in 1704, was confirmed
by the tribe, and then only through the powerful
influence of Sir William Johnson.

On the 24th day of March, 1772, three years
before the war of the Revolution broke out, and
about the time the first white settler was building
his rude cabin at the Springs, these two patents
of Saratoga and Kayadrossera, were united by
the colonial government into a district. The
name Kayadrossera was dropped, and the district
named after the smaller patent, and called the district of Saratoga. Since then the grand old Indian

name Kayadrossera, so far as territory is concern-
ed, has fallen out of human speech and is only
heard in connection with the principal stream and
mountain chain of the great hunting ground so famous in Indian history. The old hunting ground,
the beautiful lake, and the famous springs have all,
since the 24th day of March, 1772, borne the
name of Saratoga.

There is very little doubt that the mineral
waters of Saratoga were well known to the abori-
ginal inhabitants, long before they were visited
by white men, and that they employed them
as remedial agents, with the same intuition which
they have ever displayed in the discernment of
the virtues of the herbs and trees of their native
wilds.

It was not until the year 1773, six years after
Sir William Johnson's initial visit, that the first
clearing was made and the first cabin erected at
the Springs. The hardy adventurer who accomplished this brave feat was Derick Scowton. He
commenced business in the double capacity of
hotel-keeper and Indian trader. Unluckily, matters did not thrive between bold Derick and his
red neighbors, who made his new home so un-
pleasantly hot that he found it wise to abdicate,
leaving his hotel incomplete.

Derick was followed a year later, and with
better success, by George Arnold, an adventurer

from Rhode Island. Arnold took possession of
the vacated Scowton House, and "ran" it, as we
say at this day, with tolerable success, for about
two years. How many daily arrivals he had is
not upon the record, neither does history enlight-
en us in respect to his bill of fare, or his per diem.
Still, it is clear that neither one nor the other in
any way approached the ideas of our day.

The third Saratoga landlord was one Samuel
Norton, who squatted on the Scowton estate soon
after the exit of George Arnold. Norton made
various improvements, clearing and cultivating
the land around him. He might have made a
"good thing" of his enterprise, but, as ill-luck
would have it, the first mutterings of the great
storm of the Revolution just then began to greet
his terrified ears, causing him to decamp, and
thus leave the Hotel Scowton again without a
landlord. Norton was at length, in the year
1783, succeeded by his son, who, taking possession
of the old property, still further improved it,
until 1787, when he sold out to Gideon Morgan,
who in his turn and within the same year made it
over to Alexander Bryan.

Bryan became the first permanent settler at the
Springs after the close of the war. He enriched
the estate with a blacksmith's shop and an additional log-house.

The days of the Scowtons, the Arnolds, the

Nortons, the Morgans, and the Bryans were the
primitive days of very small things; indeed the
first or exploratory epoch in the settlement of the
spring region. They were followed in 1789 by a
new and more brilliant era, under the reign of
the Putnams—an era and reign which steadily
advanced from that hour and has continued,
ever expanding, down to our own days of full
fruition.

Gideon Putnam is deservedly remembered as
the father of Saratoga, by the virtue of many
and varied contributions which he made to the
growth and prosperity of the village, from his
first settlement in it, in his early youth, to his
death, twenty-three years later.   He was a
Massachusetts man, who set out in the quest of
fortune in the spirit of indomitable energy which
he never afterwards failed to display in all his
many undertakings.   .

Saratoga county was formed from a part of
Albany in February, 1791.

The town of Saratoga Springs was formed April
9th 1819, and it was made a post town April 17th
1826. In 1831 a subscription was raised to build
a railroad from Schenectady. From that time
Saratoga Springs has grown rapidly, and with
more or less steadiness. It has had its ups and
downs, its fires and hotel openings, its dull times
and its periods of wonderful prosperity. To-day
it has a population of 10,820, and offers more attractions than ever.

CHAPTER IV.

SARATOGA SPRINGS.

1886.

GENERAL NOTES.

SARATOGA SPRINGS, JUNE 1ST, 1886.—Saratoga has awakened from her winter slumber, and the preparations for the approaching season are rapidly advancing toward completion. There has been no delay nor difficulty in this extensive undertaking on account of labor strikes, the wage workers of Saratoga having wisely resolved to defer all questions relating to hours of work and compensation therefor until after the summer harvest has been reaped.

Of the hotels, the Worden, which keeps open all the year, and Dr. Strong's are already entertaining a number of early guests, many of whom have come to look out for desirable cottages to lease or to drink the spring waters without being jostled by the summer crowds.

The elegant Huestis House, on South Broadway, is also open and has a considerable number of guests.

The Windsor, as well as the Grand Union, will

this year be under the management of Mr. J. M.
Otter, who has succeeded Mr. Henry Clair in the
control of the hotels belonging to Judge Hilton
and Mrs. A. T. Stewart. The Windsor was
bought by Judge Hilton a few years ago, and he
at once made it over again in the so-called Queen
Anne style.

The Grand Union has been renovated and bur-
nished up. Lothian's mammoth Boston orchestra will play here for its eleventh consecutive season.

The Everett House is open under the proprietorship of Mr. P. M. Suarez, who has built up for it
such an extensive business, and it will be the
headquarters of our Cuban visitors as usual.
Here the black eyed senoritas and their swarthy
protectors will enjoy their national dances in a
northern clime which is for the time as sunny as
their own.

The Clarendon will have a new proprietor this
summer in the person of Mr. I. Steinfeld, of the
Hotel Normandie, New York. Puerner's orchestra, from New York will furnish the music and
play for the balls and hops at this charming
house this summer.

The Columbian, one of the cosiest houses in Saratoga, has been purchased since the close of last
season by Mr. J. M. Case, who had conducted it
so successfully during the two previous years.

The Congress Hall continues under the control of its owners, Messrs. Clement and Cox. They have made extensive improvements in this renowned caravansary, among which may be mention a thorough replumbing. The music at the Congress will be supplied by Joyce's orchestra, from New York, which gave so much satisfaction to the guests last year, and the ball room will be in charge of Mr. J. A. Mahler, of St. Louis, one of the most efficient and popular of Saratoga's "masters of ceremonies."

The American will be under the sole management of Mr. George A. Farnham, the interest of Mr. Bush having passed into his hands.

The Kensington, will open June 19. Franko's parlor orchestra has been re-engaged for the coming season.

The United States will be conducted by Tompkins, Gage & Co. as usual. Stubb's orchestra, from New York, will come up about the 1st of July.

The various suburban hotels have undergone great changes, except that at the White Sulphur Spring, on the further side of Saratoga Lake which will again be under the management of Mr. T. C. Luther. Very important changes and improvements have been made in the famous old road house on the lake shore which was kept so long by Mr. C. B. Moon, and famous for fine din-

ners, will be in new hands. It was bought last
summer by Mr. Edward Kearney, of New York,
and District Attorney John Foley, of Saratoga,
and the place has been leased by Mr. Mower, of
New York. The beautiful lake will be more than
ever a centre of attraction this year.

Of Saratoga's other suburban places of entertainment the best known is the now famous
Mount McGregor, where the great American sol-
dier closed his earthly career last summer. The
cottage in which Grant died has been presented
by its former owner, Mr. Joseph W. Drexel, to
the United States government, the Legislature of
New York having given its consent at its present
session.

One of Saratoga's road houses has undergone a
very unique transformation. This is the well
known Glen Mitchell Hotel and park, just north
of the village. Last year it was leased by the
Saratoga Toboggan Club, who erected their slide
there for use last winter. Now, however, this
sporting resort of other days has been bought by a
Roman Catholic society known as the Redemp-
torist Fathers, who are fitting it up for use as a
preparatory seminary for their college at Baltimore. The theological students in black gowns
and wide brimmed hats will present quite a striking contrast to some of the old time enjoyers of
these beautiful grounds. The school will, how-

ever, not be opened until September, when some
forty seminarians and the faculty will take possession.

While in the suburbs the extensive improvements of Mr. Spencer Trask, the well known New
York banker, at "Yaddo," his charming country
seat on Union avenue, should not be overlooked.
The cottage on this extensive estate has been enlarged until it has fairly reached the dimensions
of a mansion. The architecture is exceedingly
unique, and the noble building cannot fail to
excite admiration as well as arrest attention. A
number of other elegant cottages and country
seats have been erected during the past year, especially in the vicinity of Judge Hilton's handsome Woodlawn Park and on Union avenue,
which is the principle drive to the lake and the
thoroughfare by which the gay procession whirls
out to the park of the Saratoga Racing Association in the bright summer mornings.

Perhaps the most striking pieces of residential
architecture are presented, however, by the new
cottage of Mr. Edward Kearney, on Caroline
Street, and the stately mansion of Mr. Harry S.
Leech, also of New York, on the prominent corner of Circular Street and Union Avenue, overlooking Congress Spring Park. The last mentioned house will be one of the most conspicuous
objects that will call forth the admiration of Sar-

atoga's summer guests, with its pronounced style, great extent and graceful out-lines.

The racing prospects are very bright, the increase in the number of running horses in the country having kept fully abreast with the multiplication of tracks and stakes. The entries are up to last years figures, and all the important stakes are well filled. The season of turf sports will begin on Saturday, July 24, and continue every day, except Sundays, until August 28. The former patrons of this track, are substantially all represented in the entries, while there are many new stables in the list, the Dwyer Brothers have returned and will contest all the important events with their crack flyers. The conflict of dates has hurt the Saratoga track somewhat in recent years, but the great increase in the number of thoroughbred horses, before alluded to, has filled the fields this year, and it seems, indeed, that with no more tracks and races than this country enjoyed ten years ago it would be impossible to handle the vast fields of contestants that would face the starters flag. There will be five races each day, and they will begin at half past eleven each morning, as they did last last year. The long distance events have in recent seasons been contested by comparatively slender strings of competitors, but it looks as though the old time figures when the colors of the Lorillard's, Withers, Jerome, Belmont, Astor and others were seen upon the Saratoga course, would be exceeded this year. In the entries for the Saratoga Cup race, two miles and a quarter, for instance, appear the names of Freeland, Miss Woodford, Bersan, Bob Miles, Boatman, Editor and Modesty, all first class flyers and able to make the distance. The large number of running horses is possibly making itself felt in this direction also.

The hotel proprietors all report better lists of advance engagements than they have had for several years. But perhaps the most striking fact in connection with Saratoga's summer visitors is the increasing tendency toward cottage life. The volume of business at the great hotels and the multitude of smaller public houses steadily grows, but at the same time the movement toward more secluded and less gregarious summer life gains force each year. Judge Hilton's Woodlawn Park is being rapidly surrounded with elegant villas, and others are springing up in all the more favored portions of the village. Among the cottage residents who have built their own seats or rented from others for the season of 1886 are the following :

Ex-Minister Levi P. Morton and family.
Mr. A. M. Kalbfleisch, of Brooklyn.
Mrs. James Brown, of New York.

Mr. George Pancoast, of New York.

Mr. Ferdinand Fursch, of New York.

Mr. George C. Hammel, of New York.

Mr. H. Blum, of New York.

Mr. B. A. Haggin, of New York.

Mrs. J. E. Cameron, of New York.

Although the Saratoga outlook is the best since the great season of 1882, and, with peace and prosperity reigning throughout the country, it bids fair to surpass even that high water mark, which has been looked at with mingled regret and encouragement all through the three less successful seasons that have intervened.

EUREKA

White Sulphur Spring

HOT and COLD SULPHUR BATHS

Visitors to Saratoga will be glad to learn that in connection with the other Mineral Springs, there is a White Sulphur Spring of great purity, highly impregnated with Sulphur. For bathing purposes and curative properties, unsurpassed by any Sulphur Spring in the United States, and is highly recommended by the most eminent physicians in the country.

A large and commodius bathing house containing fifty bath rooms, and replete with every convenience for warm and cold Sulphur Baths, every care is taken to give satisfaction to visitors. Lady and Gentlemen attendants always on hand.

Trains on B. H. T. & W. R. R. stop at Eureka Station. Fare, Ten cents round trip.

Open from 6 A. M. to 6 P. M.

The Daily Saratogian,

The Leading Watering-Place Journal of the Country.

*Has been Published at Saratoga Springs for over Thirty Years,
and is well known to the thousands
of frequenters of this great
summer resort.*

It is served EVERY MORNING to guests at all the hotels and boarding houses in the place.

It contains each day a full report of all the hotel arrivals, together with the current social news, personal gossip, reports of balls, hops dinners, excursions to the lake, &c.

THE SARATOGIAN is on file during the summer season at most of the principal watering-places throughout the country, and is also sent regularly during the season to large numbers of distinguished people in all parts of the country, making it the choicest advertising medium in the country.

Specimen Copies Sent on Application.

RATES OF ADVERTISING.

Half an inch space, one month	....	$ 6 00
" " two months	....	9 00
" " three months	....	12 00
One inch, one month	....	10 00
" two months	....	15 00
" three months	....	20 00

☞Fifty per cent. extra for every additional inch or half inch. Twelve lines space make one inch.

B. F. JUDSON, Manager

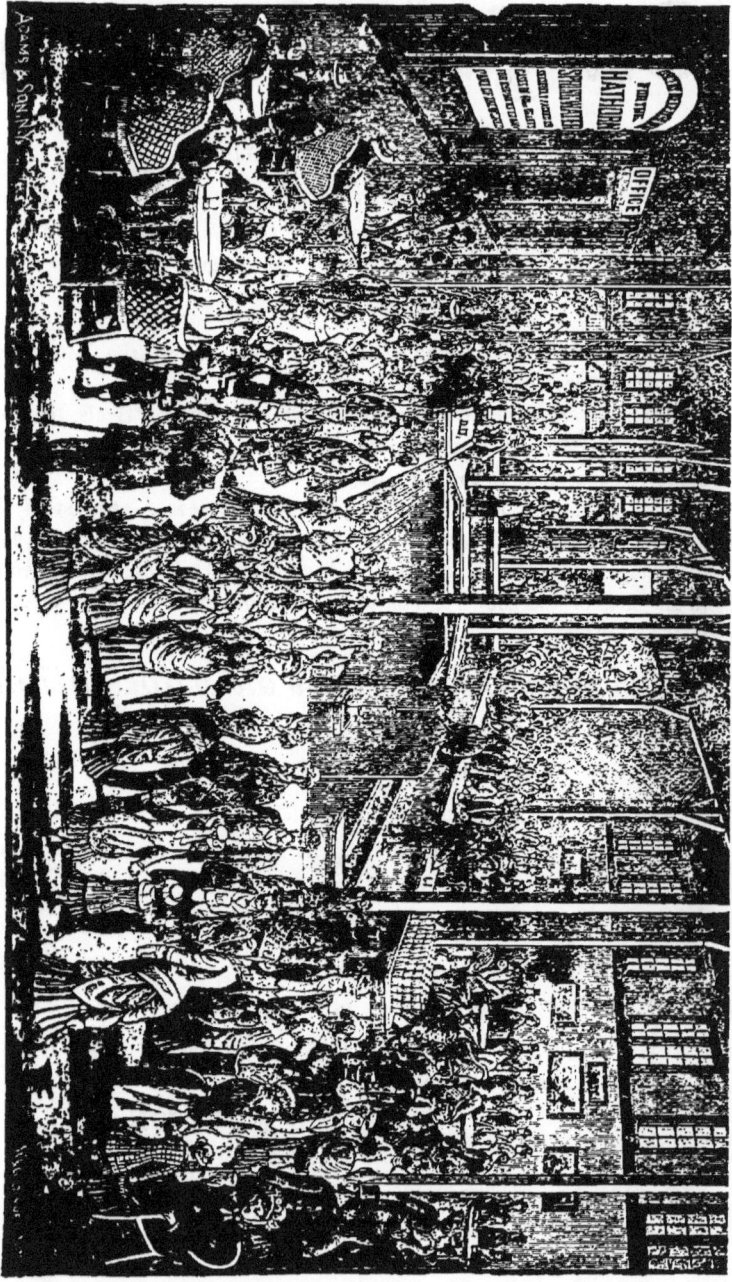
HATHORN SPRING. (INTERIOR.)

CHAPTER V.

THE SPRINGS.

"WHENCE THE ORIGIN OF YOUR MINERAL
SPRINGS ?"

This is a question often propounded by persons
who visit Saratoga, and undoubtedly, to those
who have not made the complex operations of
nature their study. There is very much of
mystery connected with this matter; that the
reader may be enabled to understand the facts
bearing upon this subject, we will state succinctly
the geological character of this locality.

In the valley in which they occur two geological systems of rocks meet and abut against each
other. Here the old Laurentian rocks, covered
by the rocks of the Potsdam and calciferous sand-
stones end, and the Trenton system of limestone,
covered by the Hudson river slates and shales,
begins. In the geological fault or fissure which
runs along the valley, between these two systems
of rocks, the mineral springs rise to the surface.
The springs seem to take their rise in the birds-
eye limestone strata, which underlies the slate.
In sinking wells, at the Geyser springs, at Ballston Spa, and at Round Lake, the mineral waters
like those of Saratoga were, without exception,

reached after the drill had passed through the
slate, and struck the limestone. At the Geyser
the wells are sunk to the depth of one hundred
and thirty-two to three hundred feet. At Ballston
Spa, they reach the depth of several hundred
feet more, while at Round Lake the well was sunk
through the slate to the depth of fourteen hundred feet, before the limestone was reached, in
which the mineral water was found. It would
seem that the valley of the Hudson, at this part
of its course, is a deep sunken basin, in which
lies a fossil ocean, in whose ancient bed the limestone and slates were deposited in its briny
waters. Out of this sunken basin of still briny
waters, out of this fossil ocean-bed filled with
rocky strata, rise the mineral springs of Saratoga. The waters course along between the
limestone strata at different depths, and therefore
possessing different qualities, until they reach the
hard barrier of Laurentian rocks in the fissure
that extends through the little valley in the village in which they occur, and then they rise to
the surface forced upwards by their gaseous constituents.

APOLLIS SPRING.—This spring is about 15 feet
from the High Rock Spring, and belongs to the
High Rock Springs Co. The water has become
very popular from its great resemblance both in
appearance and taste to the Appolinaris water.

An Analysis of the Saratoga Mineral Waters, by C. F. Chandler, Ph.D., of the Columbia School of Mines.

Compounds as they exist in Solution in the Waters.	Champion Spouting Spring.	Congress Spring.	Empire Spring.	Excelsior Spr.*	Geyser Spouting Spr.	Hathorn Spring.	High Rock Spring.	Pavilion Spring.	Red Spring.	Star Spring.	Triton Spring.	Saratoga Vichy.
Chloride of sodium	702.239	400.444	506.630	370.642	562.280	509.968	459.127	459.903	83.530	378.962	238.500	128.659
Chloride of potassium	40.446	8.049	4.292	7.000	24.634	9.597	8.497	7.660	9.299	9.229	16.980	14.113
Bromide of sodium	3.579	8.559	0.266		2.212	1.634	0.781	6.837	55.650	1.800		0.990
Iodide of sodium	0.234	0.138	0.006	4.235	0.249	0.198	0.086	0.937	8.000	0.042		
Fluoride of calcium	Trace.	Trace.	Trace.	Trace.	Trace.	Trace.	Trace.	Trace.		Trace.	Trace.	Trace.
Bicarbonate of lithia	6.947	4.761	2.080		9.004	11.447	9.486	0.942	5.199	5.199	1.760	Trace.
Bicarbonate of soda	17.624	10.775	9.022	15.000	71.232	4.283	84.388	3.764	15.397	12.662	82.878	1.760
Bicarbonate of magnesa	198.912	121.757	42.953		149.843	176.463	54.924	76.267	42.413	61.912	70.470	82.678
Bicarbonate of lime	227.070	143.399	109.656		170.646	170.646	131.739	120.169	61.912	70.470	41.503	95.522
Bicarbonate of strontia	0.082	Trace.	Trace.	Trace.	0.425	Trace.	Trace.	Trace.	Trace.	Trace.	Trace.	Trace.
Bicarbonate of baryta	2.053	0.928	0.670		2.014	1.737	1.473	0.675			0.992	Trace.
Bicarbonate of iron	0.647	0.940	0.793	3.215	0.979	1.128	1.223	2.510	2.100	1.283	0.593	0.473
Sulphate of potassa	0.252	0.889	2.769		0.319	1.260	2.960	2.033			0.052	0.753
Phosphate of soda	0.010	0.016	0.023		Trace.	0.006	Trace.	0.007	Trace.		Trace.	Trace.
Biborate of soda	Trace.	Trace.	Trace.	4.000	Trace.	Trace.	Trace.	Trace.			Trace.	Trace.
Alumina	0.468	Trace.	0.418	Trace.	Trace.	0.131	Trace.	0.329			Trace.	Trace.
Silica	0.609	0.840	1.145	1.321	0.665	1.960		3.165	1.213	1.557	Trace.	Trace.
Organic matter	Trace.	Trace.	Trace.	Trace.	Trace.	Trace.	Trace.	Trace.		Trace.	Trace.	Trace.
Total per U. S. gallon, 231 cu. in.	1195.552	710.895	680.436	514.746	991.546	888.408	625.032	697.275	254.719	615.685	544.627	367.826
Carbonic acid gas	465.458	392.289	344.669	250.000	454.082	375.747	400.458	332.458		407.550	361.500	388.071
Density	1.096	1.096	1.096		1.011	1.115	1.092	1.075				
Temperature	49°F.	52°F.	48°F.		46°F.	52°F.	52°F.	52°F.	40°F.	40°F.	40°F.	50°F.

* The Excelsior Water was analyzed by the late R. L. Allen, M. D., of Saratoga Springs.

"A" SPRING (1-16 G).—The "A" Spring is situated off Geneva street, beyond the Empire Spring, and a little north of the Red Spring, on the eastern side of a steep bluff of calciferous sand-rock. It is one of the oldest springs in Sara. toga. A fine, large bottling-house adjoins the spring.

As the merits of spring waters were so little known and understood in the earlier days of their discovery. no attempt was made to introduce this spring to public attention until 1865, when a shaft twelve feet square was sunk to the depth of six. teen feet, and the spring was first tubed. In the spring of the next year the fountain was more perfectly secured by a new tubing. In 1867 the bottling-house was destroyed by fire, and the spring after a time was again retubed to the depth of thirty-two feet, going down to the solid rock, where one of the most perfect veins of water was found flowing in all its original purity; this was secured with the greatest care, and brought to the surface through a maple tube.

The Saratoga "A" Spring water is one of the most effective mineral waters found on either continent. It has four times greater mineral properties than the Baden Baden of Austria, five times that of Aix-la-Chapelle in Prussia, twice that of the Vichy of France, nearly three times greater than the Seltzer of Germany and equally over the Spas of England and Kissengen in Bavaria.

ANALYSIS

f the Saratoga "A" Spring Water.

BY JULIUS G. POHLE. M. D.

Chloride of Sodium	565.800	grains
Chloride of Potassium	.357	"
Chloride of Calcium and Magnesia	trace.	
Bicarbonate of Soda	6 752	"
Bicarbonate of Lime	56 852	'
Bicarbonate of Magnesia	20.400	"
Bicarbonate of Iron	1.724	"
Sulphate of Lime	.448	"
Sulphate of Magnesia	.288	"
Sulphate of Soda	2.500	'
Sulphate of Potassa	.370	"
Silicic Acid	1.460	"
Alumina	.380	"

Solid contents per gallon	656.911	grains
Free Carbonic Acid Gas, per gallon	212	cubic inches
Atmospheric Air	4	"

BROOK SPRING (2-16 G).—The Brook Spring is located in Excelsior Park, near Excelsior Spring. This Spring water we understand has not been analized, the spring is not often opened and its water is not bottled. It is the property of Mr. F. W. Lawrence.

CHAMPION SPOUTING SPRING.—This most re-markable natural curiosity, which is justly considered to be the wonder among the springs of this far-famed summer resort, was dis. covered in August, 1871, by Mr. Jessie Button, and is situated on Ballston avenue, about one mile and a half from the principal hotels of the village.

After a careful observation of the surface of
the ground, the indications were such as to invite
a deeper search, which it was hoped would reveal
a hitherto unknown fountain of healing.

The work of boring was commenced and continued until the depth of three hundred feet was
reached, passing through slate rock, limestone
and magnesian lime, beneath which was found a
cavity of six inches in depth, in which the mineral water runs, and which is believed to be the
fountain head of all the mineral waters of Saratoga. On reaching this cavity the water burst
forth with great force, throwing a stream, six and
a half inches in diameter, to the height of twenty-
five feet above the orifice. The spring was then
carefully and securely tubed and cemented, that
it might be protected against any impurity from
fresh or surface water.

The Champion spring water contains a very
large preponderance of the elements which render
mineral waters valuable as a medicine, and which
are in constant use by physicians of the various
schools. It also contains a much greater amount
of carbonic acid gas than any other water, hold-
ing the valuable mineral embraced in its composition in perfect solution, thus rendering it im-
pervious to the effects of age or climate.

The remarkable cures of some of the prevailing
diseases effected by the use of Champion water has

given the waters of this spring great favor among professional men and others whose occupations are sedentary. For the disease known as clergyman's sore throat, this water occupies a deservedly high position as a curative agent. As a Cathartic, Alterative and Dieuretic, this water is unquestionably superior to all others, and is unequalled in the treatment of Dyspepsia, Biliousness, Constipation, Malaria, Scrofula, Bheumatism, and all disorders of the Blood, Liver and Kidneys.

The proprietors of this spring have erected a most handsome bottling house, over which is a large hall set apart for the convenience of visitors, where the water is dispensed by the attendant. The drive is through the Champions's own grounds, laid out in a most artistic style, and visitors are driven under a canopy, which is an appendage to the bottling house. At the back of the hall, and at an elevation of forty feet above the spring, is a broad piazza, where visitors may enjoy the sight of this wonderful natural curiosity. The following analysis of the Champion water is by Prof. C. F. Chandler, a great authority on mineral waters :

Analysis of One U. S. Gallon.

Chloride of Sodium	702.289	Bicarbonate of Baryta	2.083
Chloride of Potassium	40.446	Bicarbonate of Iron	0.642
Bromide of Sodium	3.579	Sulphate of Potassa	0.257
Iodide of Sodium	0.234	Phosphate of Soda	0.010
Fluoride of Calcium	trace.	Biborate of Soda	trace
Bicarbonate of Lithia	6.247	Alumina	0.458
Bicarbonate of Soda	17.624	Silica	0.699
Bicarbonate of Magnesia	193,912	Organic matter	trace.
Bicarbonate of Lime	227.070		
Bicarbonate of Strontia	0.082	Total grains	1195.582

Carbonic Acid Gas, 465.458 cubic inches. Temperature, 49 deg. Fah.

CHAM ION SPOUT NG SPRING IN WINTER.

SARATOGA "A" SPRING.

SARATOGA SPRINGS, N. Y.

Sold in bottles, also in Block tin lined barrels. Can
be had of most Druggists, or direct from the Spring.

SARATOGA SPRING CO.,

C. P. MITCHELL, Agent.

———— ►►◄◆►◄◄ ————

COLUMBIAN SPRING (4-4 G).—This spring is
located in Congress Spring Park, just west
of the park entrance and on Broadway. It is
one of the oldest of the mineral springs, having been opened by Gideon Putnam in 1806. It
is covered by a beautiful and artistic pavilion,
and is approached through the park entrance to
the right, or down a few steps from Broadway
opposite the Columbian Hotel. The spring is
owned by the Congress and Empire Spring Company. It is a fine chalybeate mineral water, and
possesses singularly active properties in certain
diseases.

It is said to be especially valuable in liver complaint, dyspepsia, erysipelas and all cutaneous

disorders. As a tonic water for frequent use, no spring in Saratoga is so popular as the Columbian.

The water is recommended to be drank in small quantities frequently during the day, generally preceded by the use of the cathartic waters taken before breakfast. Only from one-half to one glass should be taken at a time. When taken in large quantities or before breakfast, a peculiar headache is experienced.

The proper use of this water will strengthen the tone of the stomach, and tend to increase the red particles of the blood, which, according to Liebig, perform an important part in respiration. Though containing but 5.58 grains of iron in each gallon, this water has a perceptible iron taste in each drop. Is it much to be wondered at, then, that a mineral which has so great a power of affecting the palate should possess equally potent influence upon the whole system? The happy medicinal effects of these iron waters seem to consist, to some extent, in the minute division of the mineral properties, so that they are readily taken into the system.

Analysis of Columbian Water.

BY PROF. E. EMMONS.

The specific gravity of this water is 1007.3 ; its solid and gaseous contents as follows:

Chloride of Sodium	267.00	grains.
Bicarbonate of Soda.	15.40	"
Bicarbonate of Magnesia	46.71	"
Hydriodate of Soda	2.56	"
Carbonate of Lime	68.00	"
Carbonate of Iron	5.58	"
Silex	2.05	"
Hydro-Bromate of Potash	scarcely a trace.	

Solid contents in a gallon	407.30	grains.
Carbonic Acid Gas	272.06	inches.
Atmospheric Air	4.50	"

276.56 inches.

CONGRESS SPRING (3–5 G).—This spring is lo cated in Congress Spring Park, opposite the southern end of Congress Hall. There is an artistic and very beautiful pavillion built over it to protect visitors from the sun and rain. The principal entrance to the spring-house is at the grand entrance to the park, near Broadway. On entering the park, turn to the left, pass along the arbor-like colonade to the pavilion about the spring, where seats are provided, and the spring water drawn by a novel process, is served upon small tables by the attendants. By descending a few steps to the east, along the colonade to the cafe, hot coffee and other refreshments may be obtained. Admission to the park is regulated by tickets, for which merely a nominal charge is made.

Congress Spring was discovered in 1792, just

thirty-five years after the visit of Sir William
Johnson to the High Rock.

A hunting-party happened to observe numerous
deer-tracks, leading in a particular direction;
and, following the trail with some curiosity, to
see whither it led, they stumbled upon a new
mineral spring, which the deer, it appears, were
in the habit of visiting in their search for salt.
The water issued from a rock about three feet in
height, through an aperture midway between the
top and the ground. Among the Nimrods was a
member of Congress named Gilman, and in honor
of this gentleman and his high position, the new
fountain was christened Congress Spring.

The water was first secured by pressing a cup
against the rock, through which means not more
than one quart per minute was obtained. To increase the yield, and to economize the loss by
this primitive mode of drawing, Gideon Putnam,
who was at all times wide awake, set about clearing and tubing the spring. He first turned the
brook some few feet from its original course, and,
guided by the bubbles of gas, which rose from
the channel of the stream, he sunk a shaft into
the rock. The water thereupon ceased to issue
from the old aperture, but rose in ample supply
from the new opening, and was at once secured
as completely as was practicable, by means of a
tube made of pine planks.

INTERIOR OF CONGRESS SPRING PAVILION,
SARATOGA SPRINGS, N. Y.

The waters were at first bottled for exportation
in 1823, by Dr. John Clarke, of New York, who
purchased the spring from the Livingston family,
who held it under an ancient grant. The property was purchased of Dr. Clarke's executors, in
1865, by the Congress Spring Company, the present proprietors.

The medicinal effects of Congress water have
been tested for nearly a century, and its use is
prescribed by physicians with the utmost confidence, after long knowledge of its great efficacy,
and the entire comfort and safety with which it
may be used. To professional men and others
whose occupations are sedentary, and to all suf-
ferers from various forms of bilious disorders, it
is invaluable. It contains enough of the laxative
salts (chloride of sodium and bicarbonate of magnesia) to render its effects certain without the
addition or use of cathartic drugs; and it produces free and copious evacuations without in
any manner debilitating the alimentary canal or
impairing the digestive powers of the stomach.
At the same time it does not contain an excess of
those salts, the presence of which in the cruder
mineral waters, native and foreign, often renders
them drastic and irritating, producing very
serious disorders.

TO SARATOGA. 63

ANALYSIS BY PROF. C. F. CHANDLER.
LABORATORY OF THE SCHOOL OF MINES, COLUMBIA COLLEGE,
NEW YORK, AUGUST 17th. 1871.

The sample of Congress Spring Water, taken by me from the Spring, contains, in one United States gallon of 231 cubic inches:

Chloride of Sodium	400.444	grains
Chloride of Potassium	8.049	"
Bicarbonate of Magnesia	121.757	"
Bicarbonate of Lime	143 399	"
Bicarbonate of Lithia	4.761	"
Bicarbonate of Soda	10.775	"
Bicarbonate of Baryta	0.928	"
Bicarbonate of Iron	0.340	"
Bicarbonate of Strontia	a trace.	
Bromide of Sodium	8.559	"
Iodide of Sodium	0.138	"
Sulphate of Potassa	0.889	"
Phosphate of Soda	0.016	"
Silica	0.840	"
Fluoride of Calcium		
Biborate of Soda	each a trace	
Alumina.		

Total ....700.895 grains.
Carbonic Acid Gas.............392.289 cubic inches.

CRYSTAL SPRING (3 G).—This spring is said to have the same general character of the other springs, and to be quite as valuable as a medical agent. For some reason this spring has been closed, and the writer had some difficulty in locating it, but for those who may be curious, we may say that the floor of the first one story building, (an art gallery) on the north side of the Columbian Hotel on South Broadway, now covers what was once known as the Crystal Spring.

EMPIRE SPRING.

DIAMOND SPRING.—The Diamond Spring is north-east of the vichy, in its grounds, and is a chalybeate or iron spring, with ingredients very different from those of its near neighbor. It possesses valuable tonic and diuretic properties, and is specially recommended for those suffering from general debility.

EMPIRE SPRING (6-16 H).—This spring, one of the best in Saratoga, is located in the north part of the shallow valley that runs through the village. This spring is enclosed in a pavilion in front of the bottling-house. For full information concerning this spring, call at the office of the Empire Spring Company. Although the existence of mineral water in this locality was known for a long time it was not until 1846 that any one thought it worth the necessary expense of excavation and tubing. It was tubed by Messrs. W. & H. S. Robinson, who were the owners of the property. It then passed into the hands of G. W. Weston & Co. in 1848, who commenced bottling the water and making extensive improvements, which were continued by the next proprietors, D. A. Knowlton and the Saratoga Empire Spring Company, until it became the property of the Empire Spring Company in 1884.

The rock was struck twelve feet below the surface of the earth, and so copious was the flow of

water that the tubing proved to be a work of unusual difficulty.   When once accomplished, the
water flowed in great abundance and purity.   It
soon attracted the attention of medical men, and
was found to possess curative properties which
rendered it available in diseases which had not
before been affected by Saratoga waters.   It has
proved itself adapted to a wide range of cases,
especially of a chronic nature, and its peculiar
value is recognized by eminent medical men.   Its
general properties closely resemble the Congress,

It is especially adapted to the successful treatment of rheumatism and gout, which are certain
to be improved or cured by its use ; and all
eruptive diseases of the skin, pimples, blotches,
and ulcers, are most effectually eradicated, while
its purifying effect adds tone to the stomach,
and invigorates the whole system.   As a preven-
tive or remedy for the diseases natural to warm
climates, especially intermittent, gastric, and
bilious fevers, dysenteries, and disorders of the
liver this water is a remedy of remarkable efficacy.

The column of water in the tube above the rock
is nine and a half feet—the tube itself being
eleven and a half feet.   The fountain yields the
liberal supply of seventy-five gallons per hour.

ANALYSIS OF EMPIRE SPRING WATER.

By Prof. C. F. Chandler.

One United States gallon (231 cubic inches) of Empire Water contains:

Choloride of Sodium	506.630	grains.
Choloride of Potassium	4.292	"
Bicarbonate of Magnesia	42 953	"
Bicarbonate of Lime	109.656	"
Bicarbonate of Lithia	2.080	"
Bicarbonate of Soda	9.022	"
Bicarbonate of Baryta	0.070	"
Bicarbonate of Iron	0.793	"
Bicarbonate of Strontia	a trace.	
Bromide of Sodium	0.266	"
Iodide of Sodium	0.006	"
Sulphate of Potassa	2.769	"
Phosphate of Soda	0.023	"
Silica	1.458	"
Alumina	0.418	"
Fluoride of Calcium, ⎫		
Biborate of Soda, ⎬	each a trace.	
Organic Matter, ⎭		
Total	680.436 grains	
Carbonic Acid Gas	344.669 cubic inches.	

EUREKA SPRING.—A few yards south of the White Sulpher Spring and close to the Eureka station is the mineral Eureka Spring. This water is highly charged with carbonic acid gas, making it one of the most pleasant to the taste of all the Saratoga waters. It is a superior tonic, diuretic and mild, cathartic.

For some time this spring has been closed, but this season it will be open from 6 a. m., to 6 p. m., and will be under the management of Mr. J. P. Haskins, to whom all applications in reference to it should be addressed.

ANALYSIS.

Of the Eureka Spring.

By R. L. ALLEN, M. D.

	Grains.
Chloride of Sodium	166.811
Bicarbonate of Soda	8.750
Bicarbonate of Lime	41.321
Bicarbonate of Magnesia	29.340
Carbonate of Iron.	3.000
Iodide of Soda	4.666
Bromide of Potassa	1.566
Silica	.532
Alumina	.231
Sulphate of Magnesia	2.146
Carbonic Acid Gas	239 000
Atmospheric Air	2.000

EUREKA WHITE SULPHUR SPRING.—This valuable spring is situated about a mile east of the
village, and about a quarter of a mile west of the
Excelsior Spring. The water of this spring is used
for bathing and drinking Its curative properties
are fully established, there is a large and
very commodious bathing-house, containing fifty
baths, and supplied with every convenience for
giving warm or cold sulphur baths at all hours
of the day.   The spring supplies a very important element to the attractions of Saratoga.   The
other springs supply valuable mineral waters to
be taken internally, while the White Sulphur
waters supply that very important element of
medicinal effects produced by bathing.   Persons
afflicted with rheumatism or cutaneous diseases
always receive, positive benefit, and generally are

completly cured by using these baths. The water is very pure, containing no mineral matter whatever except sulphur. Male and female attendants are always at hand during bathing hours, and every convenience for luxurious and wholesome bathing is afforded. The trains of the B. H. T. & W. R'y Company run at short intervals from the village to the bath-house. Fare each way, only five cents, in elegant and commodious cars.

This spring water was analized by R. L. Allen, M. D., and he says in his report, "That the water of the Eureka White Sulphur Spring, is purely White Sulphur, and contains no other ingredients. It is equal to the best, and superior to most in this State."

EXCELSIOR SPRING (7-16 H) Is found in a beautiful valley, amid picturesque scenery, about a mile east of the Town Hall, and near the centre of Excelsior Park. The principal park entrance is on Lake avenue, half a mile from Circular street, or we may approach it by Spring avenue, which will lead us past most of the principal springs and the Loughberry water works, with its famous Holly machinery, by which the village is supplied with an abundance of the purest water from the Loughberry lake. Leaving the water works, we see just before us, as the avenue bends towards the Excelsior Spring, the fine summer

SARATOGA SPRINGS, N. Y.

hotel known as the Mansion House. Surrounded
by its grand old trees and beautiful lawn, it offers
an inviting retreat from the heat and dust of our
crowded cities.

The spring is covered by a tasteful pavilion,
which will be noticed just east of the little
stream, and in front of the large bottling house
beside the grove. The Union Spring is a little
northwest of the Excelsior, and but a few steps
removed. The valley in which these two springs
are situated was formerly known as the '' Valley
of the Ten Springs,'' but the present owners, after
grading and greatly beautifying the grounds,
changed its name in honor of the spring to Excelsior Park.

The tubing extends to a depth of fifty-six feet,

eleven of which are in the solid rock. By this improvement the water flows with all its properties undeteriorated, retaining from source to outlet its original purity and strength. For several years the Excelsior Spring water has steadily increased in public favor, until its sale has become very large, and it is now to be found on draught or in bottles in nearly all the principal cities and towns of the United States. We must not fail to notice the perfect and very ingenious method, invented by the proprietors of this spring, for bottling and barreling the water. In the large and well-lighted cellar of the bottling house is a circular brick vault, in whose depths the process of filling is performed. A block-tin tube conveys the water directly from the spring to this vault, at a depth of twelve feet from the surface of the ground. By hydrostatic pressure the water is forced from the main tubing of the spring through the smaller tube to the brick vault into air-tight barrels, or reservoirs, lined with pure block tin. These reservoirs contain two tubes, one of which extends from the top to the bottom of the barrel, the other being shorter. When these reservoirs are connected with the tube leading from the spring, the water is forced by hydrostatic pressure through the long tube into the barrel, and the air is driven out through the shorter tube, while the gas of the water is not allowed to escape. To draw the water from the reservoirs, it is only necessary to attach the draught tube to the long tube of the barrel, and connect the shorter one with an air-pump, when

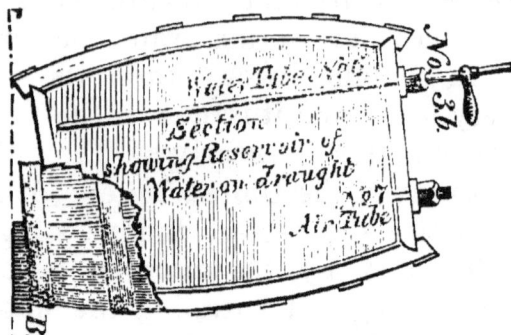

the pressure of the air will force out the water without its being recharged with gas—pure, sparkling and as delicious as though it were taken directly from the spring.

Analysis of the Excelsior Spring Water.

As analyzed by the late R. L. ALLEN, M.D., of Saratoga Springs.

Chloride of Sodium....... ....370 642 grains.
Carbonate of Lime............................. 77.000 "
Carbonate of Magnesia. .... 32.333 "
Carbonate of Soda.... .... 15 000 "
Silicate of Potassa.......... .... 7.000 "
Carbonate of Iron................................. 3.215 "
Sulphate of Soda... ....· 1.321 "
Silicate of Soda................................. 4.000 "
Iodide of Soda.............................. ..... 4.235 "
Bromide of Potassa............................. a trace.
Sulphate of Strontia... .... a trace.

    Solid contents in a gallon.................. ..514.746 grains.

Carbonic Acid,..............................250 cubic inches.
Atmosphere 3   "

    Gaseous contents........................253 cubic inches.

GEYSER SPRING.—The Geyser Spring is near Geyser Lake, about a mile and a quarter from the village.

Prof. C. F. Chandler, Ph. D., of Columbia College School of Mines, a few weeks after its discovery, made the following analysis from water collected by him at that time :

Analysis of One U. S. Gallon.

Chloride of Sodium	562.080	grains
Chloride of Potassium	24.634	"
Bromide of Sodium	2.212	"
Iodide of Sodium	0.248	"
Fluoride of Calcium	trace.	
Bicarbonate of Lithia	9.004	"
Bicarbonate of Soda	71.232	"
Bicarbonate of Magnesia	149.343	"
Bicarbonate of Lime	168.392	"
Bicarbonate of Strontia	0.425	"
Bicarbonate of Baryta	2.014	"
Bicarbonate of Iron	0.979	"
Sulphate of Potassa	0.318	"
Phosphate of Soda	trace.	
Biborate of Soda	trace.	
Alumina	trace.	
Silica	0.665	
Organic matter	trace.	

Total solid contents	991.546 grains.
Carbonic Acid Gas in one U S Gallon	454.082 cub in.
Density	1.011
Temperature	46° Fah.

HAMILTON SPRING (8-7 H.)—The Hamilton Spring is located on Spring street, corner of Putman Street.

The following ingredients were obtained from one gallon, by an analysis by Dr. John H. Steele in 1831, viz.:

```
Choloride of Sodium.........................297.3000  grains
Carbonate of Lime........................... 92.400    "
Carbonate of Iron...  .....................  5.390     "
Hydriodate of Soda..........................  3.000    "
Bicarbonate of Soda......................... 27.036    "
Bicarbonate of Magnesia.....  .............. 35.200    "
Hydrobromate of Potash......................  . trace.
Solid contents in one gallon....  .....  .........460.326  "
Carbonic acid gas..................................316.000 Cub. in.
Atmospheric air...  ...................  .........  4.000   "
Gaseous contents in a gallon....................320.000    "
```

HATHORN SPRING (9-6 G.)—This spring was discovered in the fall of 1868. In the winter of 1871-2. the mineral water vein of the Hathorn Spring was secured, as it issued from two natural openings in the Trenton Limestone Rock, by two wooden tubes about 35 feet long, covering these openings and carrying the water upward to the surface of the ground.

During the past winter the Diamond Drill has tapped the vein at two points within the rock, one boring through the rock 29 1-2 feet (depth 75 from surface,) and again in another location 60 feet through the rock (depth 118 from surface) to

reach the vein. These two drill holes have been
tubed with glass-lined iron piping, to conduct the
water from the vein to the top of the ground, thus
affording two new outlets for the spring, making
four in all.

It is on Spring Street, near Broadway, and is
named in honor of the Hon. H. H. Hathorn, who
first developed the spring, and built the famous
Congress Hall. The spring has had four tubings
the cost of which has been about $30,000. Al-
though this spring cannot compare in age with
many of the springs, yet it has attained a wide
spread popularity, and its water may be found on
sale by druggists, grocers, and hotels, in nearly
every town of note in the union. The water contains 820,844 grains of solid contents to the gallon ;
Carbonic acid gas 375.747 inches ; Density 1,009.

In the opinion of the most eminent medical men,
Hathorn Water is nature's sovereign cure for
Constipation, Dyspepsia, Torpid Liver, Inactive
Conditions of the Kidneys, and a most salutary
alterative in Scrofulous Affections. With ladies,
gentlemen and *bon vivants* everywhere, it has become the standard of dietary expedients, fortify-
ing the digestive functions, and enabling free liv-
ers to indulge with impunity at table   The world
of wealth, intelligence and refinement, testifies to
its sparkling, naturally pure and delightful qual-

ities as the beverage incomparable, and accredit it with being the surest and speediest source of clear complexions, high health and exuberant spirits.

The spring is open daily through the year; during the season from 6 A. M., to 10 P. M.

The following is the analysis by Prof. Chandler made in 1885 :

Analysis of the Hathorn Spring:

Chloride of sodium	478.722 grains.
Chloride of potassium	32.859 "
Bromine of sodium	3.644 "
Iodide of sodium	0 115 "
Flouride of calcium	trace.
Bicarbonate of lithia	7.290 "
Bicarbonate of Soda	17.635 "
Bicarbonate of magnesia	130.555 "
Bicarbonate of lime	147.226 "
Bicarbonate of strontia	trace.
Bicarbonate of baryta	0.972 "
Bicarbonate of iron	0.853 "
Phosphate of soda	0.015 "
Biborate of soda	trace.
Alumnia	0.258 "
Silica	0.700 "
Organic	trace.
Total solid contents	820.844

HIGH ROCK SPRING (10-14 G).—This wonderful mineral fountain is located on Spring avenue, from Broadway turn down Rock street in the northern portion of the village.

The High Rock is the oldest, in point of discovery, of the Saratoga springs. As early as

1767 Sir William Johnson was brought to it on a
litter by his Indian friends of the Mohawk tribe.
It takes its name from the dome shaped rock—a
superb vase of nature's unassisted workmanship
—which is justly considered the most remarkable
curiosity in the vicinity. The mound of stone,
three or four feet high, appears like a miniature
volcano. Eminent scientists estimate that the
formation of this rock has taken not less than
five thousand eight hundred and seventy years.

The High Rock Spring, which may be looked
upon as the father of all these healing waters,
has stood the test of over a century. It is a
superior tonic and cathartic, as well as alterative.
It is useful in Rheumatism, Scrofula, Dyspepsia,
Constipation, and a wide range of diseases.

Great pains have been taken, and no expense
spared, in retubing and putting in perfect work-
ing order this old, and for many years the only
known mineral spring at Saratoga. The utmost care
has been taken not only to keep out all impure
and fresh waters, but also to preserve and retain
the fixed carbonic acid gas, for which this spring
is so pre-eminently celebrated; and the proprietors
are now able to supply pure mineral water.

As an aparient or cathartic the water should be
taken in the morning, half an hour before breakfast, its temperature not over cool—same temperature as sleeping-room. For instant action
warm the water slightly.

Appended is an analysis made by Prof. C. F. Chandler, who personally collected the water for his analysis :

Analysis of One U. S Gallon of High Rock Water.

Chloride of Sodium	390 127	grains.
Chloride of Potassium	8.497	"
Bromide of Sodium............................	0.731	"
Iodide of Sodium...........	0.086	"
Fluoride of Calcium	trace.	
Sulphate of Potassa...........................	1.608	"
Bicarbonate of Baryta..........................	trace.	
Bicarbonate of Strontia........	trace.	
Bicarbonate of Lime	131.739	"
Bicarbonate of Magnesia......	54.924	"
Bicarbonate of Soda............................	34.888	"
Bicarbonate of Iron.............	1.478	"
Phosphate of Lime............................	trace.	
Alumina	1.223	"
Silica	2 260	"

Total. .... .628.039 grains.
Carbonic Acid Gas........ ....409.458 cubic inches.

MAGNETIC SPRING (14–16 G.)—The Saratoga Magnetic spring is situated on Spring avenue. It is unlike all other springs in Saratoga, having that wonderful magnetic influence, which is one of the great marvels of nature.

Its valuable qualities are recognized by physicians and residents of Saratoga, and has added another and peculiar. feature to this wonderfully rich mineral spring region.

MINNEHAHA SPRING (11–15 H.)—This spring is located a few rods east of the Excelsior spring.

PAVILION SPRING (12–10 G.)—The Pavilion is located between Caroline street and Lake avenue, one block east of Broadway.

Analysis of Pavilion Water.

Chloride of Sodium	459 903	grains.
Chloride of Potassium	7 660	"
Bromide of Sodium	0.987	"
Iodide of Sodium	0.071	"
Fluoride of Calcium	trace.	
Bicarbonate of Lithia	9.486	"
Bicarbonate of Soda	3.764	"
Bicarbonate of Magnesia	76.267	'
Bicarbonate of Lime	120.169	"
Bicarbonate of Strontia	trace.	
Bicarbonate of Baryta	0.875	"
Bicarbonate of Iron	2.570	"
Sulphate of Potassa	2.033	"
Phosphate of Soda	0.007	"
Biborate of Soda	trace.	
Alumina	0.329	"
Silica	3.155	"
Organic matter	trace.	

Total... ...687.275 grains.

Carbonic Acid Gas, 332.458 cubic inches. Density, 1.0075, contained in U. S. gallon of 231 cubic inches.
August 9, 1869.   C. F. CHANDLER.

PUTNAM SPRING (13-9 G).—The Putnam spring is located on Phila. street, one block north of Hathorn spring. The new Putnam is used for drinking purposes, and will bear favorable comparison with many of the more noted springs. The old Putnam is mainly used for bathing purposes. Suitable rooms and every convenience will be found at the Phila. street entrance.

This spring was tubed in 1835 by Mr. Lewis Putnam

Analysis of the Putnam Spring,

```
Chloride of Sodium ...........................220.000 grains
Carbonate of Soda . ...... ...........  ....... 15.321   "
Carbonate of Mag esia ............. ... ..... .. 45 500   "
Carbonate of Lime  ..... ................ .......... 70.433   "
Carbonate of Iron...........···· .... ............  5.333   "
Iodide of Soda ............ ................ ....... 2.500   "
Silex and Alumina.........  ..........  ..... 1 500   "
```

```
    Solid contents.... ................... ..360.587 grains.
Carbonic Acid ....................... ....317.753 cubic inches.
Atmospheric Air........................... 3.080      "
```

```
    Gaseous contents.... .................320.833 cubic inches.
Temperature ........................... 48 deg.
```

RED SPRING (14–16 H.)— This spring is located on Spring Avenue. It was discovered in 1770.

The following is the analysis of the Red Spring Water, made by Prof. John H. Appleton, of Brown University, R. I. The amounts specify the number of grains of the various substances in one imperial gallon of the water.

```
Bicarbonate of lithia...............Lio, HO, 2, CO;   .942 grains
Bicarbonate of soda.... ...........NaO, HO, 2, CO;  15.327   "
Bicarbonate of magnesia ...........MgO, HO, 2, CO;  42.413   "
Bicarbonate of lime ...............CaO, HO, 2, CO; 101.256   "
Chloride of sodium............ ..NaCl,              85.530   "
Chloride of potassium .......... .. KCl,             6.857   "
Alumina and sesquioxide of iron....... ............  2.100   "
Silica ...............................................  3.225   "
Phosphates.................... ....................  a trace.
```

```
    Total ... ......................................254.719 grains.
```

SELTZER SPRING (10-14 G).—The Seltzer Spring
is close to High Rock Spring, and in the neighborhood of the Star and Empire. Although in
such close proximity thereto, its water is entirely
different, thus illustrating the wonderful extent
and capacity of nature's subterranean laboratory.

Analysis of Seltzer Water.
BY C. F. CHANDLER, PH. D.

In one gallon of 231 cubic inches are contained:

Chloride of Sodium	134.291	grains
Chloride of Potassium	1.335	"
Bromide of Sodium	0.630	"
Iodide of Sodium	0,031	"
Fluoride of Calcium	trace.	
Bicarbonate of Lithia	0.899	"
Bicarbonate of Soda	29.428	"
Bicarbonate of Magnesia	40.339	"
Bicarbonate of Lime	89 869	"
Bicarbonate of Strontia	trace.	
Bicarbonate of Baryta	trace.	
Bicarbonate of Iron	1.703	"
Sulphate of Potassa	0.557	"
Biborate of Soda	trace.	
Pmosphate of Soda	trace.	
Alumina	0.374	"
Silica	2.561	"

Total	302.017	grains.
Carbonic Acid Gas	324.08	cubic inches

Temperature of Water Spring, Saratoga, 50° Fah·

STAR SPRING (16-15 G.)—This spring, situated
about midway between the High Rock and Empire springs, was formerly known as the President and later still as the Iodine. It is over half
a century since its waters were first known and

used, but their full virtues were not developed until 1862, when the water was traced to its rocky sources, and the spring tubed in the best manner. In 1880 it was retubed, the tubing carried forty-four feet into solid rock, securing perfect freedom from surface waters,

Since then the Saratoga Star spring has greatly increased its popularity as a mineral water, and is now recognized as one of the leading waters in the principal markets. The water is largely

charged with carbonic acid gas, which renders it peculiarly valuable as a bottling water, since it preserves its freshness much longer than waters containing a smaller amount of gas.

While the immediate effects of the Star water are cathartic, in remote effects are alterative, and these, after all, should be considered the most important, as the water thus reaches and changes the morbid condition of the whole system, giving the Star water the high repute which it has maintained from its first discovery. For the following complaints it has been used with marked advantage: scrofula, cutaneous eruptions, bilious affections, rheumatism, gravel, calculus, suppression, fevers, dyspepsia, constipation, diabetes, kidney complaints, loss of appetite and liver difficulties. Owing to the great amount of iodine with which the water is charged, it was always held in high esteem by invalids, especially those suffering from chronic rheumatism, scrofulous complaints, cutaneous eruptions, etc.

The following analysis was made at different times, extending over a period of thirty years, by Prof. C. F. Chandler ; also by Dr. Steele and Prof. Emmons. The result shows that the great medicinal properties of the Star water consist in the large quantity of iodine and bromide of sodium, being two grains of iodine and fourteen grains of bromide to each quart.

Analysis.

Chloride of Sodium	878.962	grains.
Chloride of Potassium	9.229	"
Bromide of Sodium	55.650	"
Iodide of Sodium or Iodine	8.000	"
Sulphate of Potassa	5.400	"
Bicarbonate of Lime	120.549	"
Bicarbonate of Magnesia	61.912	"
Bicarbonate of Soda	12.662	"
Bicarbonate of Iron	1.213	"
Silica	1.283	"
Phosphate of Lime	trace.	

Solid contents in a gallon.................615.685 grains.
Carbonic Acid Gas, 407.55 cubic inches in a gallon.

NEW STAR SPRING.—Mr. D. H. Porter, proprietor of the Star spring, has had drilling operations going on for some time in close proximity to the Star spring, hoping to tap a vein of mineral water that would gush up into a veritable "geyser." A depth of 212 feet was reached, at which an entire new vein was struck, and although it rises no higher than the surface of the earth, it seems to be inexhaustible. It is of an excellent quality, and in some respects unlike any other of the numerous mineral waters which have made Saratoga famous. An expert water taster said in describing it: "It is less saline than the Empire, strongly impregnated with gas, and of the excellent flavor of the Vichy." This sprihg has not interfered with the "Star" in the least, although only four feet apart. The water is now being analyzed by Prof. C. F. Chandler, of the Columbia School of Mines, New York, who is considered to rank A 1 in his profession, and who has analyzed nearly all of the Saratoga mineral waters, his report is expected in a few weeks and the general expectation is that this water will be classed as an alkaline water.

TRITON SPRING.—On the east side of the Geyser Lake.

The following analysis, made by Jas. R. Nichols & Co., Boston, in 1872, gives the amount of ingredients, named in grains, of one U. S. gallon of 231 cubic inches :

Analysis of Triton Spring Water.

Chloride of Sodium	238.500	grains.
Chloride of Potassium	16.980	"
Bromide of Sodium	1.800	"
Iodide of Sodium	0.042	"
Fluoride of Calcium	trace	
Bicarbonate of Lithia	5.129	"
Bicarbonate of Soda	67.617	"
Bicarbonate of Magnesia	70.470	"
Bicarbonate of Lime	40.260	"
Bicarbonate of Strontia	trace.	
Bicarbonate of Baryta	0.992	"
Bicarbonate of Iron	1.557	"
Sulphate of Potassa	trace.	
Alumina	trace.	
Silica	1.280	"
Organic matter	trace.	

Total solid contents in one U. S. gallon........544.627 grains.
Temperature........................... 40 deg. Fah.
Density............................ 1.0060
Cubic inches CO2 in one gallon............361.5
Total residue by evaporation................432.634

UNION SPRING (17-16 H).—The Union Spring, is about ten rods northwest of Excelsior Spring, and was originally known as the Jackson Spring. The water was, however, but imperfectly secured until the present proprietors had the spring retubed in 1868. The water of the Union Spring acts as a mild cathartic when taken before breakfast. Drank at other times during the day, it is a very agreeable and healthful beverage. The water is of excellent strength, the ratio of magnesia to lime being unusually large, and an almost entire absence of iron. The water is bottled and put up in barrels similar to the Excelsior water; the spring being the property of Mr. F. W. Lawrence, the proprietor of the Excelsior.

A ..ysis of the Union Spring Water.

BY PROF. C. F. CHANDLER.

Contains in one U. S. Gallon of 231 cubic inches:

Chloride of Sodium	458.299	grains
Chloride of Potassium	8.733	"
Bromide of Sodium	1.307	"
Iodide of Sodium	0.039	"
Fluoride of Calcium	trace.	
Bicarbonate of Lithia	2.605	'
Bicarbonate of Soda	17.010	"
Bicarbonate of Magnesia	109 685	"
Bicarbonate of Lime	96.703	"
Bicarbonate of Strontia	a trace.	
Bicarbonate of Baryta	1.703	"
Bicarbonate of Iron	0.269	"
Sulphate of Potassa	1.818	"
Phosphate of Soda	0.026	"
Biborate of Soda	trace.	
Alumina.	0.324	
Silica	2.653	"
Organic matter	trace.	

Total solid contents..................701.174   "
Carbonic Acid Gas in one gallon.. ....384.969 cubic inches.
Temperature............................. 48°F.

UNITED STATES SPRING (12-10 G).—This spring is located in United States Park, five feet from Pavilion Spring, though the two springs are entirely different. It is covered with the same handsome pavilion. While excavating for the purpose of retubing the Pavilion spring in 1869, a new spring, flowing from the east, was discovered. This has been tubed, its waters analyzed, and they are now presented to the public. This water is more gentle in its action and more tonic in its effects. As a tonic, from a half to two tumblers several times during the day is necessary.

Analysis of United States Water.

Chloride of Sodium	141.872 grains.
Chloride of Potassium	8.624 "
Bromide of Sodium	.844 "
Iodide of Sodium	.047 "
Fluoride of Calcium	a trace.
Bicarbonate of Lithia	4.847 "
Bicarbonate of Soda	4.666 "
Bicarbonate of Magnesia	72.883 "
Bicarbonate of Lime	92.119 "
Bicarbonate of Strontia	.018
Bicarbonate of Baryta	.908 "
Bicarbonate of Iron	.714 "
Sulphate of Potassa	none
Biborate of Soda	trace.
Phosphate of Soda	.016 "
Alumina	.094 "
Silica	3.184 "
Organic Matter	a trace.

Total ....331.837 grains.
Carbonic Acid Gas 245.734 cubic inches.—Density 1.0035, contained in U. S. gallon of 231 cubic inches.

August 9, 1869,   C. F. CHANDLER.

FLAT ROCK SPRING.—This spring is situated
east of the Town Hall, on Lake Avenue, and is
one of the oldest of the many mineral fountains
of Saratoga. It is stated on the authority of residents of Saratoga, in 1774, that the Flat Rock and
High Rock springs were the only ones then known.
The Flat Rock covered a quantity of ground
several rods in extent. It was considerably elevated above the marsh or swamps which surrounded it. The surface was flat and hard, and was
perforated in numerous places where the water
stood in little pools, through the bottom of which
it was constantly bubbling up. The marsh and
grounds about the rock were much broken and
trodden up by the footsteps of wild animals which
flocked here in great numbers to drink the water.

Some of the older citizens of Saratoga can remember the time when about four o'clock in the
afternoon a procession of people, with their pails
and pitchers, might be seen going from this spring,
laden with spring water with which to make spring
water biscuit.

In those days spring water lemonade, foaming
and sparkling, was the regulation drink of a hot
afternoon, and the fashionable guests from the
elegant Pavilion Hotel made it their daily resort.

But by injudicious digging the vein was lost,
and it fell into neglect and disuse for a long period.
In the spring of 1884, Mr. Reuben Merchant, who

owned the property, employed Mr. John B. Hall,
a veteran spring digger, to search for the long lost
vein. A pit was dug sixteen feet square and forty
feet deep, to the solid rock, when the vein was
found, after which it was thoroughly tubed and
brought to the surface.

On the first of August it was thrown open to the
public, and at once found its old time popularity.
its Analysis, made by Prof. C. F. Chandler, of
Columbia College, which is appended, shows it to
be an Alkaline water; that is, the Soda, Magnesia,
Lithia, &c., predominate over the Chloride of
Sodium or Salt.

It is found highly efficacious in Kidney Troub-
les and Impaired Digestion.

In its constituent elements it resembles the celebrated Vichy more nearly than any other water.

ANALYSIS.

Grains in one U. S. gallon of 231 Cubic inches.

Chloride of Sodium	108.845
" " Potassium	7.989
" " Magnesium	10.835
Bromide of Sodium	0.323
Iodide " "	0.011
Bicarbonate of Lithia	3.233
" " Soda	9.098
" " Magnesia	29.466
" " Lime	98 635
" " Strontia	0.009
" " Baryta	0.103
" " Iron	0.086
Sulphate of Potassa	0.479
Phosphate of Soda	0 037
Biborate of Soda	trace
Alumina	0 040
Silica	1.341
Organic Matter	trace
Carbonic Acid Gas	370.900
Density. Temperature 48°	

VICHY SPRING —The following is the analysis, made by Prof. C. F. Chandler, of Columbia College School of Mines.

Analysis of Vichy Water.

Contained in one U. S gallon of 231 cubic inches.

Chloride of Sodium	128.689	grains.
Chloride of Potassium	14.113	"
Bromide of Sodium	0.990	"
Iodide of Sodium	trace.	
Fluoride of Calcium	trace.	
Bicarbonate of Lithia	1.760	"
Bicarbonate of Soda	82.873	"
Bicarbonate of Magnesia	41 503	"
Bicarbonate of Lime	95.522	"
Bicarbonate of Strontia	trace.	
Bicarbonate of Baryta	0.593	"
Bicarbonate of Iron	0.052	"
Sulphate of Potassa	trace.	
Phosphate of Soda	trace.	
Biborate of Soda	trace.	
Alumina	0.473	"
Silica	0.758	"
Organic matter	trace.	
Carbonic Acid Gas in one gallon	383.071 cubic inches.	
Temperature	50 deg. Fah.	

WASHINGTON SPRING (18-3 G).—The Washington spring is within the grounds of the Clarendon Hotel, on South Broadway. It is a chalybeate or iron spring, having tonic and diuretic properties. It is not a saline water, and the peculiar inky taste of iron is perceptible. It should be drank in the afternoon or evening, before or after meals, or just before retiring One ·glass is sufficient for tonic purposes. Many

LAWN VIEW, VICHY SPRING, SARATOGA.

regard this as the most agreeable beverage in Saratoga. Its lively and sparkling character has acquired for it the name of the "Champagne spring." It is a very popular spring, and in the afternoon is thronged with visitors. Its grounds are very picturesque, and in the evening are lighted with gas.

For dyspepsia, all affections of the kidneys, dropsy, chronic diarrhœa, general debility, and all those irregularities and distressing diseases known only to the female sex, it will be found to produce the most beneficial effects.

Analysis of Washington Spring Water.

By JAMES R. CHILTON & Co., Practical Chemists.

	Grains.
Chloride of Sodium	182.733
Bicarbonate of Magnesia	65.973
Bicarbonate of Lime	84.096
Bicarbonate of Soda	8.474
Bicarbonate of Iron	3.800
Chloride of Calcium	0.203
Chloride of Magnesium	0.680
Sulphate of Magnesia	0.051
Iodide of Sodium	2.243
Bromide of Potassium	0.474
Silic Acid	1.500
Alumina	trace.

	Grains
Grains	350.227

The gases contained and analyzed at the spring yielded for the gallon as follows :

Carbonic Acid	363.77
Atmospheric Air	6.41

Cubic inches	370.18

APPEARANCE OF THE WATERS.—When first
. dipped from the spring the water is not unlike lemonade in appearance, and that from the
spouting springs is like cream soda, both in color
and action. The gas, however, quickly escapes,
and the water has a wonderful purity. When
allowed to stand some time, however, the water
becomes cloudy, a filmy skin forms on the surface
and in time a reddish precipitate is formed.

DISEASES AFFECTED BY THE WATERS.—The
medicinal virtues of the Saratoga waters are of a
rare and very varied character, efficacious in the
treatment of many troublesome complaints, and
invaluable to the partial invalid and all generally
dilapidated and used-up visitors, as a pleasant
and sure cathartic and tonic. Taken in reasonable quantity and particularly in connection with
the fresh air, exercise, physical and mental re-
pose, and the pleasurable recreations incident to
the routine of Saratoga life, the waters never fail
to provoke appetite, promote digestion, exorcise
the blues and the bile, and to generally purify,
strengthen and cheer both body and mind. For
a detailed and scientific account of their properties and virtues in relation to the various classes
and stages of disease, in the cure and correction
of which they may be used, to give a list in detail would be useless and confusing, and perhaps
harmful. There is but one course to pursue in

drinking the spring waters for the health's sake : Consult a resident physician, let him make a diagnosis of your case, and under his advice select the particular spring of most value to you, and govern yourself in all things by his experience and acquaintance with the waters. The medical staff of Saratoga Springs is excellent, and one may rely on their ability to assist and direct.

Concerning the directions for their use, much the same thing may be said. As well try to give advice in making prescriptions for the general public. Each user of these healing waters must, in a measure, be a law unto himself. To drink any and all of the waters would be simply un- reasonable. Seek proper advice, and then follow it, and be not led aside by the enthusiasm of some invalid who, having been restored to health by some particular spring, thinks it a cure for all diseases, whether they are allied to his special case or not. To persons in perfectly good health, the waters do no particular harm, even if in- dulged in freely. At the same time, there is reason in all things, and if one is really unwell, there is but one thing to do—consult a medical man.

The late Dr. Steel wrote, in 1837 : "The waters are so generally used, and their effects so seldom injurious, particularly to persons in health, that almost every one who has ever drank of them assumes the prerogative of directing their use to others. Were these directions always the result of careful experience and observation, they would be less objectionable, but there are numerous persons who flock about the springs, without any positive knowledge of the composition and effect of the waters, who contrive to dispose of their directions many times to the detriment of those who desire to be benefited, but who are thus disappointed in the use of the water."

PROPERTIES OF THE WATERS.—These are almost as varied as the fountains from which the mineral waters flow. Cathartic, tonic, alterative and diuretic, magnetic and sulphur water, of various shade and differing strength are found in Saratoga. Each spring has its own peculiar virtues that adapt it to certain forms of disease. Hence, it follows that mineral waters should not be drank promiscuously, but under the direction of a competent physician, who thoroughly understands the composition and peculiarities of each, if the utmost benefits would be obtained. Many imagine that if the waters do no good they certainly do no harm. This is a mistake, and one which may result in serious injury.

The first taste of the waters is not always lovely. After the first blush, the water becomes exceedingly enjoyable and one is tempted to indulge too freely in the pungent, acidulous and salty mixture. The after-effects resemble those of soda-water, and, if a large quantity is taken, there follows a sense of fullness, perhaps a slight giddiness in the head and a desire for sleep.

The most important ingredients of the Saratoga waters are natural to the body, and are also powerful oxydizers of the disintegrated tissues, carrying out of the body the waste matter. Mineral waters are similar to the blood, minus its organic constituents, and are true restorative medicines, as well as powerful modifiers of the tissues themselves; and these properties, and their gentle mode of action, constitute no small degree of their extraordinary merit.

"Saratoga water is a cholagogue in its properties; that is, it stimulates the action of the liver, and promotes the excretion of bile. Certain matters are secreted by that organ, which, if allowed to remain in the system, produce such diseases as jaundice. A great number of intestinal diseases and blood disorders are associated with derangements of the the

The waters are not only laxative or aperient, but are are also diuretic, antacid, desobstruent, alterative and tonic.

They increase the force of the heart and arteries, promote digestion, favor the action of the nutrient vessels, increase the peristaltic movement of the bowels, cleanse the system through the granular organs, and impart strength and vigor."

TEMPERATURE OF THE WATER.—The springs vary from 46° Fah. to 52° Fah., but the difference of temperature between summer and winter is scarcely preceptible and is said not to vary more than 1° in the whole year. In the very warmest weather the waters are all cool and agreeable.

BOTTLING AND PACKING THE WATERS.—The bottling and packing is carried on throughout the year. The arrangements for this purpose are the most complete of anything of the kind in the country, and all the various operations are carried on with a care, skill and perfection unsurpassed.

In order to increase the facilities for obtaining bottles, the Congress and Empire Company erected a good glass-house sometime since, and now, not only this company, but many of the others are easily supplied with such bottles as they need. Some of the bottles are dark glass, and others, like those used by the Geyser Spring Company, are of white or crystal glass.

The bottles are securely packed in wooden boxes, and every box is fully marked to prevent all mistake. Each box contains two dozen quart or four dozen pint bottles.

The waters are either pumped through block-tin pipes from the springs, or the water is forced into the bottles by its own hydrostatic pressure. When pumps are employed, a large receiver is used to hold the water under pressure and free from contact with the air, and in drawing it the utmost care is taken to prevent the escape of the gas held in the water. In the case of the pipe wells, the water is drawn like so much soda-water into the bottles from pipes that tap the main wells many feet below their outlets.

The corks, after being soaked in warm water until they become so soft as to be easily compressed, are driven into the bottles by machinery, the process reducing their size before entering the bottles about one-third. It requires a strong bottle to stand the pressure of their expansion after being driven in, and even strong men sometimes find it difficult to pull them out. A single workman will fill and cork from fifteen to twenty dozen bottles per hour.

When the bottles and corks have been thoroughly tested, the corks are securely wired, this operation being performed with great rapidity by employees long trained to the work.

The proprietors of the springs are always pleased to show the wonders of their bottling plant to visitors, and an instructive hour may well be spent in them.

The rows of men and boys, bare-armed before the steaming washing tubs; the salt-encrusted receivers, and the bottle-filler with dextrous fingers loading up the pints and quarts; the corker, with his queer machinery; the huge bins of full and empty bottles, piled in countless

THE COLUMBIAN SPRING PAVILION IN CONGRESS SPRING PARK,
SARATOGA SPRINGS. N. Y.

thousands, one over the other; the curious in-
dustry of the wire-boys and packers, and the
vast caverns of the storage cellars, all unite to
make a scene of singular interest, and the intelligent visitor should make it a point to see at least
one of these immense establishments. The ex-
port of spring water in casks is somewhat different. The casks are of the best oak, and are
securely lined with pure block-tin.

There are two openings in these casks at the
top, and to each is secured a block-tin pipe. One
pipe extends nearly to the bottom of the cask,
and the other is only an inch or two long. In
filling the cask the water pipe from the spring is
screwed to the top of the larger pipe, and the
water, under the pressure of its gas, flows in and,
driving the air out of a small air-hole, fills the
cask. When it is full, the air hole is stopped up
but the pressure is continued for a moment or two
longer, so that the cask is not only filled solidly,
but is packed, so to speak, and the water is under
the same pressure in the cask as in its native
spring. In these casks the waters are readily
transported to all parts of the country. In
drawing the water, a block-tin pipe, with a suitable cooler, is attached to the longer pipe, and a
small air-pump to the shorter pipe. On pumping
air into the cask, the water flows out through an
ordinary soda-fountain faucet in its native
purity.

CHAPTER VL

HOTELS.

From the time when the old pioneer, Gideon Putnam, built the first seventy feet of the present Grand Union Hotel in the year 1802, Saratoga has been amply furnished with accommodation for man and beast. The late Congress Hall, which stood opposite Putnam's "Great House," almost rivaling it in extent, was commenced in 1811, also under the direction of the worthy founder of the village. It was opened to the public in 1815, and was destroyed by fire in 1866. The third of the grand hotels of Saratoga, the late United States, was commenced by John Ford in 1823, and extended in 1825. It afterwards passed into the hands of Marvin & Co., under whose management it gained the reputation of being one of the most excellent and most fashionable, as it was one of the most capacious, establishments of the kind in the country.

This trio of grand hotels, the Grand Union, the Congress and the United States, became famous all the country through, and for many years continued to divide between them the patronage of the ever-increasing throng of visitors to the Springs, and year by year they added new laurels to the reputation of the village as a place of convenient and pleasant resort.

Many other smaller, though scarcely less excellent establishments, have grown up from time to time, and have been well sustained. Saratoga has to day the largest hotels in the world ; the most perfectly appointed and the best conducted. The business is an art in which the most artful engage, and in which world-wide fame has been earned and worthily borne. It is here that the wealth and fashion of the whole country assemble, and where all the luxuries of a city home or the palace of a foreign nobleman can be found, and that, too, within a minute's walk of the healing springs.

It is this that has caused the village to open its doors so freely, and to build up, from a small beginning, a system of hotels unlike anything else to be found ; and from year to year the hotels have grown, expanding their wings, and adding room beyond room, till they cover acres of ground, and the halls and piazzas stretch out into miles. They have a bewildering fashion here of repeating the wondrous tale of these things. They talk about the miles of carpeting, the thousands upon thousands of doors and windows, the hundreds of miles of telegraph wires, vast acres of marble floors, and tons of eatables stored in the pantries, till one is lost in admirable confusion. it is all true, and that is the wonder of it. The management that governs it all is more remarkable than the gilding and mirrows. It is a sort of high science, unequalled in the world, combining the "ease of mine in" with a perfection of detail and freedom from friction that is as pleasant as it is wonderful.

CLARENDON HOTEL (25-3, F, G).—This hotel is located on Broadway, a short distance south of the Grand Union Hotel, and opposite the Windsor, with one of the pleasantest sights in the village. It partly encloses within its wings a depression or valley, ornamented with shady trees, in which stands the tasteful pagoda covering the popular Washington Spring. The halls, parlors and dining-rooms are large, and furnished with taste. The rooms are arranged for families, in suites, as their guests are of a class that do not wish to mingle with the general class of boarders at large hotels.

The Clarendon is most agreeably situated, embowered in a shady grove. Its outward presentment is very agreeable, while its inward appointments fulfil all the requirements of a first-class house. It ranks in all respects, except in size age and long service, with the United States, Union and the Congress, and is frequented by some of the very best families that visit Saratoga. The music at the Clarendon this season will be

The Clarendon,

SARATOGA SPRINGS, NEW YORK.

Open June 19th, under entire New Management.

I. STEINFELD, Prop.

by the 5th Ave. Theatre Orchestra, of New York, under the leadership of Mr. Puerner, a musician of acknowledged ability, who will give concerts twice a day ; there will also be the Clarendon Ball which is always rigidly confined to evening dress. The Clarendon is owned by Mr. I. Steinfeld, an experienced hotel man. It will accommodate five hundred guests.

THE COLUMBIAN (26-4 G.)—The Columbian, which is situated on Broadway, opposite Congress Spring Park, has been purchased by Mr. James M. Case, who has conducted the house for the last two years. A more beautiful and central location is not to be found in Saratoga. It is free from noise, homelike, and patronized by good society. The house is built of brick and has a frontage of one hundred and twenty-one feet on Broadway, with a wide' two-story piazza, one hundred and fifteen feet long, overlooking Congress Park and the fashionable drive of the town. The back piazza, one huudred and fifteen feet long, overlooks its own beautiful grounds and those of the Clarendon Hotel, including Washington Spring, and as one of these piazzas is always shaded, a pleasant retreat is furnished every hour of the day. All the rooms have pleasant outlooks, and are well furnished It will accommodate two hundred and fifty guests. The Columbian has been thoroughly renovated and new bath rooms added. The rates will be $3 per day, and from $15 to $21 per week.

COMMERCIAL HOTEL (26-9 D.)—This hotel is at the corner of Railroad place, Woodlawn Avenue and Church streets. Accommodation for 100 guests. Rates $10 to $14 per week, transients $2 per day. This hotel is close to the depot, and is open all year. Bar, Stable and all conveniences. Bryant & Wandell, proprietors.

EMPIRE HOTEL (30-15 G).—The Empire Hotel is on the corner of Rock and Front streets, and in close proximity to the Empire, Red, Star, High Rock and other springs.

This hotel again comes under the proprietorship of Mr. T. S. Estabrook who has long been favorably known in connection with it. It has recently been enlarged, improved and refurnished, having now a capacity for the comfortable accommodation of one hundred guests. Among its recent improvements are bathing rooms and modern plumbing, rendering its sanitary condition perfect. Rooms can be had en suite or single. Terms moderate. Connected with the hotel are spacious lawns, croquet grounds, carriage house and stables. For further particulars, address Mr. T. S. Estabrook, proprietor.

EVERETT HOUSE (32-G).—The Everett House is situated on Broadway a few doors south of the Clarendon Hotel, in one of the most quiet and beautiful portions of Saratoga village. Two rows of beautiful shade trees extend along side of

CONGRESS HALL.

The Columbian,

On South Broadway, between the Grand Union and the Clarendon, and opposite to Congress Park.

NEWLY FURNISHED AND SUPPLIED WITH ALL MODERN IMPROVEMENTS.

Rates $3 per Day, or $15 to $21 per Week.

JAMES M. CASE, Owner and Proprietor.

Also Proprietor Pulaski House, Savannah, Georgia.

–Season 1886.–

EMPIRE HOTEL,

IMMEDIATE VICINITY OF

OLD RED, EMPIRE, STAR,
AND HIGH ROCK SPRINGS,

AIRY ROOMS—En-suite and single.

TERMS MODERATE.
Special Terms by the Week or Month.

T. S. ESTABROOK, - Proprietor.

Corner Front and Rock Streets,
SARATOGA SPRINGS, N. Y.

Broadway at this point, and afford a delightful shady retreat on the piazza of this quiet, home-like house. The proprietor, Mr. P. M. Suarez, does not aim to attract much transient custom, but his guests are mainly families, or persons who visit Saratoga seeking quiet, health and real comfort, and who remain some months at this great watering place. During the past year another house has been added to the Everett on the south, thus giving many more rooms. The rates still remain the same—$2·50 to $3 per day and from $12 to $20 per week. This house will accommodate 200 guests.

EARL'S HOTEL—The Earl's Hotel is very near the depot, and only one block from Broadway, standing as it does on the corner of Church Street & Woodlawn Avenue. It has accommodation for 50 guests, and the rates are reasonable. Open all year. Bar, Stable, Livery, &c. M. Earl and J. Staats are the proprietors.

HOLDEN HOUSE. —Mr. C. H. Holden, proprietor, is situated on Broadway, three doors north of the United States Hotel, in the most central part of the village, and near all the principal springs. It is built of brick and can accommodate 100 to 125 guests. Its central location and moderate prices make the Holden House a very desirable hotel for visitors who seek real comfort without extravagance. The proprietor takes pleasure in informing his patrons and friends that the house is now ready for the entertainment

of guests for the season of 1886. For terms
apply to C. H. Holden.

HUESTIS HOUSE.—This popular house opened
for its twenty-first season on May 23d, with accommodation for 150 guests. The house is furnished in modern style, rooms single or en suite,
well ventilated and supplied with the best electric
annunciators, bath rooms, telephone, and other
modern improvements. The parlors are large and
handsomely furnished.

Steam heat has been introduced and extended
throughout the house, so that the cool and rainy
days never bring the chilly air to any part of the
establishment. Many of the rooms are also supplied with open wood fire places. The dining
room is very commodious and cheerful, and will
seat over 100 guests. The children's ordinary
supplies a separate dining room for children and
nurses. The cuisine is excellent, and the mode
of service unexcelled. For further particulars,
address Mr. W. B. Huestis, Manager.

IRVING HOTEL.—This is an addition to the Saratoga hotels. It is situated at 441 Broadway,
between Division and Church Streets. It is kept
open all the year, and will accommodate 75 guests.
The rates are from $2 to $2.50 per day. This
hotel has been newly furnished throughout
and no better beds are to be found in Saratoga.
The proprietors are hotel men of experience,

and everything will be done by them for the convenience and comfort of their guests. This hotel is supplied with all modern improvements, and is conducted on both American and European plan. For further particulars, apply to Burrows & Moore, proprietors.

NEW YORK HOTEL (41–10 G.)—This Hotel is on Lake Avenue, corner of Spring avenue, and facing the Pavilion and United States springs. It is open all year. Has accommodation for 70 guests. Rates: from $7 to $14 per week; transients, $2 per day. The house has a large piazza, bar, and stable for 25 horses. It is very central, only one block from Town Hall. L. J. Gorham., proprietor.

SPENCER HOUSE (42–7 E).—The Spencer House is directly opposite the depot of the D. & H. C. Co., where all trains from New York arrive. It also fronts on Woodlawn Ave., and on the south faces the United States Hotel on Division street. The house is very central, well furnished, and is kept open all year. It has accommodation for 100 guests. Rates are $2 per day, and from $8 to $12 per week. The house has been renovated since last season, and is now prepared to receive its quota of guests. Mr. N. Waterbury is the proprietor.

INTERIOR COURT VIEW OF UNITED STATES HOTEL, Saratoga Springs, N. Y.

T. H. S. PENNINGTON,

U. S. HOTEL PHARMACY,

400 BROADWAY, SARATOGA,

(Opp. U. S. Hotel and Division Street.)

PENNINGTON'S NORWEGIAN TROCHES.

The reputation which this valuable remedy has all ready gained, establishes its claim as an effective agent in diseases peculiar to the bronchial passages.

To those affections peculiar to public speakers and singers it is especially applicable, removing the dry, husky state of the throat, and allaying the irritating cough.

The Norwegian Balsam forming the basis of this combination is composed entirely of extracts from medicinal herbs and plants, which are simple in themselves, yet in combination possessing active remedia properties.

SPECIAL ATTENTION GIVEN TO

PHYSICIANS' PRESCRIPTIONS AND FAMILY ORDERS.

A Choice and Well Selected Stock of

Pure Drugs, Chemicals, Perfumery, Toilet Articles, &c.

The Worden (22-7 F).—This hotel is situated on the corner os Broadway and Division street, directly opposite the United States Hotel. It is one of the best constructed hotels in Saratoga. The building is of brick, and is of modern and improved arrangement in its interior plan, having been built but a few years. It is five stories high, surmounted with a mansard roof, and presents a very neat and attractive exterior on the fashionable avenue of the town. The house fronts two of the most prominent streets—Broadway and Division street, and its rooms are particularly desirable, as they command views of the liveliest portions of Saratoga and the business centre of the town. Extending the whole length of the Broadway front is a fine, broad piazza, two stories high, from which an extended view of Broadway may be had. Since last season considerable improvements have been made and new furniture added. The hotel is scarcely two minutes' walk from the depot, and is open the year round ; the house will accommodate 300 guests, the rate being $3 per day. For further particulars, address W. W. Worden, proprietor.

WINDSOR HOTEL

SARATOGA · SPRINGS · N.Y

THE WORDEN.

MOST CENTRAL LOCATION IN SARATOGA.

Broadway corner Division Street,

Opposite U. S. Hotel.

NEWLY FURNISHED THROUGHOUT.

Open the Year Round.

TERMS MODERATE.

W. W. WORDEN, Proprietor.

HUESTIS HOUSE,

SOUTH BROADWAY,   *Saratoga Springs.*

Open for the 21st season May 23

Handsomely Refurnished. Steam heat, Electric bells and all modern improvements. For terms and particulars address

W. B. HUESTIS, Manager.

EVERETT HOUSE,

Saratoga Springs, N. Y.

Large airy connecting rooms and baths. $2 to $3 per day.

Special rates to families. Location unsurpassed.

ON BROADWAY,   Proprietor and Manager.
NEAR CONGRESS SPRING.   **P. M. SUAREZ.**

CHAPTER VII.

BOARDING HOUSES.

Although the hotels in Saratoga are among the finest in the world, and the capacity as great, yet they are unable to provide accommodations for the vast number of visitors. Hence the problem, "How are we to entertain these visitors," and it has been solved by the creation of a number of Boarding houses, varying in size from the small cottage to the large mansion, the capacity for entertaining guests ranging from 10 to 200. Many of these houses have beautiful lawns for croquet and out-door sports, and are under competent management.

BATES HOUSE.—This house is at 109 Circular street, one of the most fashionable streets of Saratoga. It is a well conducted house, and stands high in the estimation of visitors. It has accommodation for sixty-five guests, and its rates are very reasonable, house open from June 1st to November 1st. It has large piazzas, ample shaded ground with lawn tennis and croquet grounds, all modern improvements, the rooms are high, well ventilated and elegantly furnished. C. S. Bates & Son are the proprietors.

BERNARD HOUSE. —A first-class boarding house situated on the westerly side of Franklin street,

BATES HOUSE, CIRCULAR STREET.

and having a well shaded piazza on both north
and east; has accommodation for seventy-five
guests, and is well patronized by New York, New
England and Philadelphia families. The house
is under experienced management, and every ef-
fort is made to secure the comfort of its patrons.
S. E. Benedict is the proprietor.

BROUGHTON HOUSE.—This House is at 47 William, corner of Federal street, the rooms of which
are well furnished and ventilated. The accommodation is for 50 guests, and the rates $2 per
day or $10 per week; open May to November.
The house is an old established one, is only two
blocks from Broadway, and not far from the
springs; has garden, croquet lawn, bar, billiards,
barber's saloon, &c. J. C, Broughton, is proprietor.

CIRCULAR STREET HOUSE (54–10 I).—This house
is located on Circular Street, near Phila, a first-
class boarding house with all modern improvements, open from June to October, near large
hotels and principal springs, commanding an elegant view of this avenue, with beautiful croquet
and garden plots, will accommodate seventy-five
guests. John Palmer, proprietor.

THE CONTINENTAL HOTEL is centrally located
on Washington street, west of Grand Union Hotel,
and within five minutes' walk of the principal
springs and hotels. This hotel has large and airy

rooms, well shaded piazzas, and is under the experienced management of M. E. & C. R. Knapp. During the past winter the Continental has been put in complete order, and rooms en suite can be furnished for families, which are also very convenient for transient guests. Satisfactory accommodations at reasonable prices.

COLUMBIAN PLACE, corner Broadway and Lake Avenue; open all year; accommodation for fifty guests; rates $10 to $14 per week, according to rooms; transients, $2 per day. Reduced rates out of season. The house is heated by steam, has water on every floor, and is supplied with all modern conveniences. Mrs. Mary Lemon Weston, proprietor.

ELMWOOD HALL (58-11 G).—This house is nicely located on Front Street, facing Grove Street, directly opposite the Vermont House and in close proximity to the Town Hall, the High Rock, Empire, Star, Red and Magnetic springs, and only one block from Broadway, the chief thoroughfare of Saratoga. The rooms are large and pleasant, the table is supplied with all the necessaries of a good boarding house. The house stands in its own grounds, has croquet lawns, &c., and will accommodate sixty guests. Mr. Emory Potter, the proprietor, is most assidious in his attention for the comforts of his guests. The terms are very reasonable, being from $7 to $12 per week

GRAND UNION HOTEL, SARATOGA.

according to rooms. The house is open all the
year. For further particulars address Mr. Potter,
Elmwood Hall, Saratoga.

FRANKLIN HOUSE.—The new and commodious
Franklin House on Church street, is now open
for the season under the popular management of
L. L. Brintnall. The house, which has been a
favorite summer resort during past seasons, has
been rebuilt and provided throughout with all
modern improvements. It is three stories high.
A large double parlor occupies the whole front of
the first floor, while the corresponding rooms
on the east are fitted up for family apartments.
Each floor of the house is provided with bath
rooms and closets and is well appointed in all
particulars. The dining room is large and well
ventilated. A wide, two story piazza extends
along the entire front of the house and is well
shaded. It is needless for us to mention the table
of this house as its reputation is too well known
to many of the guests that frequent Saratoga.

HOWLAND HOUSE.— Is an excellent boarding
house at 573 North Broadway, opposite the
Waverly Hotel and Mt. McGregor Railway Depot. It is one of the finest boarding houses in
Saratoga, and is in the most charming part of the
most beautiful avenue of the village. The house
has a very fine piazza fronting Broadway and
commanding a delightful view. The proprietor,

Mr. J. Howland, is one of Saratoga's most respected citizens, and has had several years' experience in catering for summer boarders.

MANSION HOUSE.—A favorite summer hotel, is situated in the midst of the beautiful Excelsior Park, and within a few rods of Excelsior and Union springs. Many well known families of our great cities spend the summer months here, attracted by its proximity to these widely known and valuable springs, as well as the beauty of its situation, and the superior style in which it is kept. The Mansion House is surrounded by a large and handsome lawn, well shaded with tall forest trees, with wide piazzas and fine tennis and croquet grounds. The house has been greatly improved this year, and thoroughly renovated as well as newly furnished throughout, and under its new management we doubt not will become more than ever popular.

NEW ENGLAND HOUSE.—This house is situated on Woodlawn Ave., No. 125, and in an elevated locality. From this house a nice view can be obtained of the surrounding country; only one block from Broadway, and within a few minutes' walk of the principal springs. The house has large piazzas, garden, &c., and is shaded. Rates are $1.50 to $2.00 per day for transients, and regular boarders $6 to $10 per week. The house is well furnished, and is kept open all year. Reduced

rates prevailing out of season. For particulars
address Dr. O. Ford, proprietor.

LAKE SIDE PLACE.—This first class boarding
house is at Saratoga Lake, and enjoys a charming
prospect. It is only a short distance from the
Lake House, stands in its own grounds, overlooking the Lake connected with the house is a
quantity of ground, orchard, &c., also separate
cottages for such as desire them, and is indeed a
first class place for families. The accommodation is for about 75 guests, and the rates are from
$10 to $12 per week. The house is open from
May to November, and is under the management
of Mrs. Luther Abel & Sons.

NIMS HOUSE.—This is a new house on Church
Street, near the corner of Lawrence. It is kept
by a gentleman, who has been connected with
hotels in Saratoga for many years, and has a
reputation for keeping a first class house. The
accommodation here is for about 40 guests, transient rates are $2 per day, and regular boarders,
$7 to $10 per week. In connection with the
house is a bar, stable, livery &c. The house is
in a good location, only one block west of depot
is well furnished and supplied with modern convenience. Mr. C. H. Nims is the proprietor.

PRESTON HOUSE.—This boarding house is at
72 Washington Street, a very desirable part of
Saratoga, being in a retired district, yet within

TEMPLE GROVE SEMINARY.

one block of the depot, United States and Grand
Union Hotels, and of the principal springs. The
house has been newly decorated and furnished,
will accommodate about 50 guests, the rates
being from $2 to 2½ per day, and from $8 to $14
per week. The Preston is supplied with gas,
water and all modern conveniences, and when it
is known that it is kept by Mr. W. J. Riggs'
late of Broadway Hall, it is unnecessary to say
that it will be well kept, or that guests will be
well cared for. Mr. Rigg's name being a sufficient
guarantee.

WASHBURNE HOUSE.—This is the seventh season of this house. It is located on Washington
street, near Broadway, and overlooks the Park of
the Grand Union Hotel. It is very convenient to
the principal springs. This is a large house, having no less than 350 feet in length of piazza, is
beautifully shaded, and has a large lawn. The
house is finished in good style, well furnished,
and is suppled with all modern improvements,
including steam heat. Table and appointments
are first class. Accommodation can be had for
125 guests ; open May to November. Major A.
S. Washburne is the proprietor.

CHAPTER VIII.

PRIVATE BOARDING.

A great number of visitors desiring more retired accommodation while in Saratoga, than can be found either in the hotels or boarding houses, Private Boarding Houses have been established. Some of the houses are very imposing, are furnished in the very best style, have all modern improvements, keep good tables, and are very desirable stopping places for visitors or families desiring pleasant surroundings, with homelike comforts at moderate rates.

31 *Caroline Street·*—This house has been renovated and undergone several alterations since last season; it is now prepared to receive its guests; accommodation from ten to fifteen; rates are from $7 to $8 per week. This house keeps open all year, and makes a reduction in its rates before and after the season. Mrs. Robert Gillis is the proprietor.

55 *Phila Street.*—This house is on the corner of Henry Street, and only two minutes walk from Broadway, Hathorn or Congress Spring. This is a good boarding house and will accommodate forty five guests. The rates are $2 per day, or from $3 to $14 per week. The house is open all year, has large piazzas, both front and side, gar-

den, &c. It has undergone several alterations
and improvements since last year, being now replete with all modern improvements and in first-
class condition for the reception of guests. Mrs.
T. D. Carpenter is the proprietor.

57 *Phila. Street.*—This is a good and old established house; it is furnished in good style and
has all modern improvements; piazza on two
sides, lawns, &c. The house can accommodate
50 guests; the rates being from $10 to $15 per
week, and transients $2 per day. Mrs. J. P.
Scovill is the proprietor.

103 *Circular Street.*—This good boarding house
is at the corner of Phila and Circular Streets, one
of the best parts of Saratoga. It is only two
blocks from the Grand Union Hotel, Congress
Park, and the principal springs. The house is
nicely shaded, has piazza, &c., and is open all
the year. The accommodation is for about thirty
guests, and the rates during the season are from
$10 to $15 per week, a reduction being made for
other parts of the year. Mrs. M. A. Magee is the
proprietor.

121 *Lake Avenue.*—This house is one of the
most desirable and pleasantly situated of any in
Saratoga; is open all the year, and has accommodation for about fifteen guests. The rates are
from 10 to 12 dollars per week; transients $1.50 to
$2 per day; reduced rates before June and after

September. The house is supplied with all modern conveniences, and is surrounded with large grounds, with garden, fruit, shade and ornamental trees; is located opposite the north end of Regent street, looking down said street between its beautiful shade trees for a long distance, also overlooks a fine private park. Stables and carriage room, and carriage belonging to the proprietor, which can be used by visitors at reduced rates. Mr. R. Churchill is the proprietor.

157 *Woodlawn Ave.*—This house is in a very quiet street, but within a few minutes walk of the Hathorn and Congress Springs and the big hotels; has accommodation for twenty guests. Rates from $10 to $12 per week; transients $2 per day. The house is well furnished and only a short distance from the depot. Mrs. M. A. Gurney is proprietor.

495 *Broadway.*—This modern house is on Broadway, opposite the 1st Presbyterian Church, and is patronized by a good class of visitors, is open all the year, and has accommodations for 30 guests. Rates are from $12 to $17.50 per week, transients, $3 per day ; the house is supplied with all modern improvements. For further particulars apply to Mrs. L. B. Putnam, proprietor.

CHAPTER IX.

MEDICAL INSTITUTIONS.

The institutions for the special treatment of diseases in Saratoga are few, but one or two are recognized by the medical fraternity as quite superior, and are certainly well supplied with medical appliances, and are under competent management.

DR. STRONG'S REMEDIAL INSTITUTE.

This excellent Institution is a popular summer resort, open all the year for boarders or patients, both permanent and transient. It is pleasantly located on Circular Street, one of the most beautiful avenues of Saratoga, within five minutes' easy walk of the great hotels, Congress Spring Park, Hathorn, and other principal springs and sources of attraction. It is just retired enough for rest, and just near enough to all the whirl. The Institution has the table appointments and elegance of a first-class hotel. Its bath department

DR. STRONG'S REMEDIAL INSTITUTE,

No. 90 CIRCULAR STREET,   —   SARATOGA SPRINGS, N. Y.

compares favorably with the best metropolitan establishments, and offers the only opportunity in Saratoga for obtaining Turkish, Russian, Roman, electro-thermal baths, massage, etc. Abundant facilities are afforded for recreation and amusement, comprising organ, pianos, parlor entertainments, fine croquet and tennis grounds, gymnasium, etc. A marked and very pleasant feature of the house is its genial, cultured society and homelike sociability. It is the summer resort of many eminent persons for rest and recreation. Among its many patrons are Rev. Theodore L. Cuyler, D. D., Brooklyn; Rev. Chas. F. Deems, D.D., New York; Rev. Jos. R. Kerr, D. D., New York; Rev. Franklin W. Fisk, D.D.; Rev. C. C. McCabe, D.D.; Rev. Dr. Potts, Toronto, Canada; Rev. J. M. Bulkley, D.D., *Christian Advocate*; Rev. Dr. Jos. Monfort, D.D., *Herald and Presbyter;* Rev. B. K. Pierce, D.D., *Zions Herald;* Bishops Foster, Warren, Robertson and Foss; Presidents McCosh, Warren, Paine, Tuttle, Hitchcock, Hamlin; Ex-Governors Wells of Virginia, Page of Vermont, Boardman of West Virginia; Judges Reynolds of Brooklyn, Drake of Washington, Bliss of Missouri; Professors Austin Phelps, D D., T. Sterry Hunt, LL.D , Cantab; Medical Professors Ross of Chicago, Knapp of New York, and many others.

A casual observer would not suspect its medical character from anything seen in or about it, as there is no appearance of invalidism, and its prominent features are those of a first-class family hotel. The advantages of a well regulated hygienic institution, so completely equipped, and under the able management of regularly educated physicians, are obvious even to those who only wish to derive the greatest benefit from a judicious use of the mineral waters.

DR. ROBERT HAMILTON'S MEDICAL INSTITUTE (4 C) on Franklin street, is an institution for the treatment of various chronic and special diseases, and is conducted by one of Saratoga's most eminent physicians, who has long enjoyed a good reputation as a practitioner, and is a conscientious student of medicine. Many are familiar with his institution that stood on the corner of Broadway and Congress street for many years, but was burned in the disastrous fire that swept away the Park Place and Crescent Hotels.

➤In the spring of 1874, Dr. Hamilton removed to Franklin street, one of the most quiet and beautiful streets in town, and has now one of the best institutions for the treatment of various diseases. He is one of the most reliable consulting physicians in Saratoga county, and having long resided and practiced in Saratoga, and observed the vari-

ous spring waters on different constitutions and in different diseases, is qualified to give advice to those who wish co drink the mineral waters in a systematic way and to the best advantage. Dr. Hamilton makes a specialty of this practice, and is recognized as a most excellent authority on the subject.

The institution is open as a summer boarding-house during the season, is kept in good style, and in such a manner that no features of a medical institution are observable. The terms are very reasonable, and all the medical patrons will be most conscientiously and ably treated, and the pleasure guests cared for with faithful attendance to their wants. We append a notice that appeared in the *Saratoga Sun*, April, 1874, which shows how Dr. Hamilton is regarded at home by those who know him best :

"Up to the time of the destruction of 'The Crescent' by fire, there was probably no medical institute in Saratoga better known or so well known as the one kept by Dr. Robert Hamilton. His common-sense method of treatment, his thorough acquaintance with the medical properties of the waters of all the springs, and the general tone of health, vigor, hopefulness and social comfort which distinguished his practice, made his institute popular with all its inmates, and famous throughout the land. It is **conveni** ently located on Franklin street, in the most quiet, genteel, and accessible part of the village, and'.those who desire to avail themselves of the excellent methods of treatment, and the superior advantages of his institution, will do wisely to make early application."

Dr. Hamilton has accommodation for 75 guests, the rates being from $10 to $20, according to rooms occupied, reduced rates out of season, and refers to some of the most distinguished visitors to Saratoga.

DR. O. FORD'S MEDICAL INSTITUTE. This Institution, which is conducted as an Eclectic Medical Institute, is situated at 125 Woodlawn Ave., (the New England House), and is also a regular summer resort. Dr. Ford has all the appliances for the cure of chronic diseases of all kinds, especially kidneys, liver, cancer and rheumatism. Dr. Ford will also attend patients staying at other houses, and give advice to visitors upon the drinking of the various mineral waters.

Dr. Ford has had upwards of forty years' experience, and has all kinds of baths at the Institute, sulphur, vapor, galvanic; also electricity in its various forms. Address Dr. Ford, 125 Woodlawn Avenue, Saratoga Springs, N. Y.

The Saratoga Sanitarium is at the corner of Walton Street and Woodlawn Avenue.

EUREKA WHITE SULPHUR SPRING.—This valuable spring is situated about one mile east of the village, and about a quarter of a mile east of the Excelsior Spring. The curative properties of it are fully established, and there is a large and very commodious bathing house, containing fifty baths, and supplied with every convenience for giving warm or cold sulphur baths at all hours of the day. The spring supplies a very important element to the attractions of Saratoga. The other springs supply valuable mineral waters to be taken internally, while the White Sulphur waters supply that very important element of medicinal effect produced by bathing. Persons afflicted with rheumatism or cutaneous diseases always receive positive benefit, and generally are completely cured by using these baths. The water is very pure, containing no mineral matter whatever except sulphur. Male and female attendants are always at hand during bathing hours, and every convenience for luxurious and wholesome bathing is afforded.

The trains of the B. H. T. & W. Railway Company run at short intervals from the village to the bath-house. Fare each way, only five cents, in elegant and commodious cars.

This spring water was analyzed by R. L. Allen, M. D., and he says in his report, "That the water of the Eureka White Sulphur Spring is purely white sulphur, and contains no other ingredients. It is equal to the best, and superior to most in the State."

CHAPTER X.

WALKS.

Saratoga Springs has quite a number of pleas.
ant and entertaining walks, and the visitor can,
if so disposed, find ample opportunities for exercise; the first, of course, is :—

BROADWAY.—The entire length of this fine
street is more than three miles in a direct line,
and even in the more thronged portions the crowd
is lost amidst the verdure of the double line of
beautiful trees which traverses the whole promenade; or the varied hues of the gay attire, con-
trasted with and seen, here and there, amidst the
green foliage, produces still a feeling of rural
rather than of metropolitan life. Much of the
street, also, is at all times quiet and country-look-
ing, for the hotel and business quarters occupy
only a comparatively small part. This quarter,
as far as it extends, is gay enough, with the showy
shops of the migratory modistes, and the other
appendages of a fashionable watering place, su-
peradded to the local business of the village. To
all this, is to be added the throngs which lounge
on the broad piazzas of the hotels, or which are
coming and going to and from the many springs.
Broadway is one entire street, yet you will be re.

minded in various ways that there is a Broadway, a North Broadway, and a South Broadway. Broadway proper is that part of the street lying between Division street on the north and Congress street on the south. From Division street a pleasant walk is along North Broadway to

WOODLAWN PARK.—This park is the private property of Judge Hilton, but through his liberality these beautiful grounds, comprising some 300 acres, are thrown open to visitors and residents of Saratoga. It is laid out in walks and drives, seven or eight miles in extent, and the paths winding over the lawn and through the shaded groves of forest trees, offer inviting retreats of entrancing beauty that should entice all lovers of nature.

Another is to take South Broadway. Just beyond the Everett House Ballston avenue turns off diagonally to the right. From this point we can turn either way and wander through quiet streets lined with beautiful and costly houses, each half-buried in its shrubbery and gardens; or forward on South Broadway to

THE CEMETERY.—A village cemetery is always an object of as much interest to the stranger as to the resident, though from different feelings and different points of view. The one resorts to its quiet haunts to read over again the changeful chapters in his own past life, and to recall memories of absent mates and friends; while the other finds there curious hints and histories of the people among whom his interests and sympathies are, for the moment, cast.

CIRCULAR STREET.—Is the fashionable residential street of Saratoga, and along which are some beautiful specimens of architecture; the houses are large and well built, and surrounded by handsomely laid out grounds.

Another walk, quite as pleasant, and may be productive of some amusement, is to take a walk to the various springs.

Other walks may be taken at will, with no fear of losing the way, as the towers of the great hotels serve as guide-marks in every direction.

CHAPTER XI.

DRIVES.

The beautiful scenery of Saratoga affords the visitor many pleasant drives to the numerous points of interest in the vicinity. Among the most enjoyable of these is the drive to Saratoga

Lake. A trip to "the Lake" would be a pictorial necessity to all Saratoga visitors, even if it were not, as it is, the terminus of the principal and most convenient "drive" from the village, and only some five miles away.

It is a lovely water in every aspect, not grand in its characteristics, to be sure, but replete with quiet and gentle beauty. It is, too, of very commanding proportions, having a liberal length of nine miles, and a breadth, in its widest division, of nearly five miles. Many and varied scenes of beauty occur within this broad range of water and shore. The boldest feature of the lake is the elevation to be seen on the right, and familiar to visitors as "Snake Hill." It may be reached by the little steamer which plies between the Lake House and the Sulphur Spring.

FOUR-AND-SIX-IN-HAND COACHES.—Not the least of Saratoga's attractions is the ride on these coaches, starting from 375 Broadway at 10 A. M. and 4 P. M. each day. These six-in hand coaches go through the entire length of Broadway, twice passing through Woodlawn Park by special permission of Judge Hilton, and down Broadway, take the road to Saratoga Lake, through Circular street to Union avenue, thence dashing along that wide and well-kept thoroughfare, leaving the village behind us, we come to the Race-course, passing Yaddo, the beautiful seat of Mr. Spencer Trask, and we emerge on the level, where a short spin brings us to the Lake House.

LAKE HOUSE.

THE STEAMBOATS

"JAMES H. BRESLIN" and NELLIE C. PRICE" & TALLY-HO COACHES can be chartered at any time by giving two-hours' notice to J. C. SLORAH, Proprietor of Tally-Ho and Omnibus Line, office 375 Broadway, Saratoga Springs.

N. B.—These two elegant Steam Yachts are new, and were built and fitted up with especial care for safety and comfort, and are provided with temperate and experienced officers.

For particulars and how to get to the Lake with ease and speed, apply to J. C. Slorah, Proprietor of the Tally-Ho Coaches and Omnibus Line, 375 Broadway, Saratoga, whose Tally-Ho Coaches and Stages always connect with the Boats.

Refreshments on board, if desired.

This is one of the most delightful trips to be found around Saratoga.

Fish and Game Dinners a Specialty

HENRY S. MOWER, Prop.

Late of Gilsey House, St. James Hotel, and Victoria, New York City.

WHITE SULPHUR SPRING PARK & HOTEL.

First-Class Accommodations.   SARATOGA LAKE, N. Y.

Special attention given to Breakfast and Dinner Parties.

FISH AND GAME SERVED IN THEIR SEASON.

Steamboat and Railroad Connections with Saratoga.

MRS. ANNA C. MYERS, formerly of Cedar Bluff Hotel. Manager.

T. C. LUTHER, Proprietor.

Telephone and Telegraph Connections with All Points.

PRIVATE BOARDING.

LAKESIDE PLACE.

SARATOGA LAKE.

Pleasant location, good rooms : good table, terms reasonable. Boarding and livery stable on the place, also laundry. Furnished cottages to rent for the season.

Also, a new Cottage and two acres of ground for sale on the bank of Saratoga Lake.

Address MRS. LUTHER ABEL & SONS, Proprietors.

P. O. Box 33, Saratoga Springs, N. Y.

THE "LAKE HOUSE," SARATOGA LAKE —This is one of the standard institutions of Saratoga, and no one who has not been there can be truly said to have seen Saratoga. The Lake House is situated on a grassy bluff, about fifty feet above the lake, from which a beautiful view of its waters may be obtained. It has no resident boarders, the proprietor catering principally to the loads that flock there to enjoy his faultless dinners, for among other things the house is noted for its fish and game dinners, and its inimitable fried potatoes.

The Lake House is connected with Saratoga by Mr. Slorah's omnibuses and his six-in-hand coaches, but in addition to these, hundreds of con- veyances may be said daily to drive with their loads to the lake ; nor are the attractions wanting when you get there, for if sailing be your fort you can go on board two of the finest yachts in the Union, or have a sail boat by the hour, or a row boat, of which there are twenty-five ; there are bowling alleys and shooting galleries, splendid bathing in the lake, or if fishing is your delight you will be provided with tackle, and when your fish are caught you may have them cooked in marvelous style, and served either on the green sward or the piazza with fried pota- toes, that have become famous throughout the Union. During some parts of the season sculling

and racing matches take place on the lake. The
steam yachts can be chartered by private parties
at any time on two hours' notice, and moonlight
trips on the lake, with bands of music, is quite a
feature in Saratoga's rounds of pleasure. There
are plenty of sheds for horses. A half-mile track
or driving park, open to all, and in fact everything that will conduce to make a visit pleasant
and enjoyable.

The six-in-hand coaches leave 575 Broadway
at the same hours every day for Woodlawn Park,
the private residence of the Hon. Henry Hilton,
who has kindly allowed Mr. Slorah the privilege
of driving through and affording visitors a view
of one of the finest parks in this State. Two
more invigorating drives than these it would be
almost impossible to devise, and visitors should
vail themselves of the privilege. For fares, &c.,
see daily papers and advertisements in this book.

A beautiful drive is through Excelsior Park,
the western entrance of which is at the intersec-
tion of East and York Avenues (near Lake Ave.),
a little over half a mile east from the Town Hall.
Here we find the commencement of a lovely shady
walk, bridle path and carriage drive through fine
old woods.

SPOUTING SPRINGS.—There are regular stages
to these springs situated about a mile and a half
from the village, round trips, 25 cents; or you

can take a private carriage, or you can walk, the
latter will probably do you the most good. The
best time to go is the latter part of the afternoon, as the Champion Sping gives its regular
performance at five o'clock every day except
Sunday. Turning off Broadway and wending
our way along Ballston avenue, we soon emerge
upon the open fields; then we come to the new
village that has sprung up about the strange
group of springs that has here been discovered.
A number of rather startling signs point the way
to the various springs.

The Triton Spring is on the Geyser Lake. From
the lake we pass on towards the Vichy Spring.
The Geyser Spouting Spring stands directly opposite the lake, and a few rods from the road.
Crossing the railroad embankment by a foot-path,
we enter the romantic valley where stands the
Champion Spouting Spring.

BALLSTON SPA is the county town of Saratoga
county, and is seven miles south of Saratoga
Springs. The drive is through Ballston avenue,
past Geyser Spring, following by the side of the
railroad to Ballston village. It is a very pretty
town of about four thousand inhabitants, with
beautifully-shaded streets and several objects of
interest to the tourist.

CHAPMAN'S HILL.—Is about a mile beyond
Moon's Lake House, and is one hundred and

eighty feet above the level of the lake, and from which the visitor can gaze upon a panorama well worth seeing.

WAGMAN'S HILL.—About three miles beyond Chapman's Hill, in a general northeast course, lies the yet loftier elevation call Wagman's Hill. It offers a charming view in all. directions, and presents a motive for a moderate excursion, either to commence or to close the day; or it may be put in as a postscript and taken pleasantly by moonlight. The return trip may be made by Stafford's Bridge.

LAKE LOVELY.—Not a great distance from the village, and accessible by way of Union avenue.

WARING HILL.—From Waring Hill the spectator will look down upon the villages of Saratoga, Ballston, Mechanicville, Schuylerville, Schenectady, and Waterford, with many other less important hamlets and settlements.

STYLES' HILL.—Styles' Hill may be reached in a drive of a few miles from the springs. To the intelligent observer the country around will recall many a thrilling recollection of historic story and romance; for it is, to those who know it, all hallowed ground.

THE PROSPECT HILLS OF GREENFIELD.—These hills are about three and a half miles northwest of Saratoga Springs. The view of the Green Mountains is very fine, and, to the south, the Helderberg Hills of Albany and the Catskills.

GROVE VIEW. TEMPLE GROVE.

CHAPTER XII.

EXCURSIONS.

The average visitor to Saratoga does not care for the constant bustle of Broadway and the hotel piazzas, and often desires a change from the somewhat monotonous, though exciting life of the springs. In the following pages we propose to give a list of beautiful spots to which excursions may be made from Saratoga, occupying generally one day, or at the most two. These excursions will bring the visitor into very romantic surroundings, green fields, grand old mountains, wild dells dancing waterfalls, fragrant woods, and the real beauty of hillside country life.

MOUNT MCGREGOR.—This delightful mountain resort is connected with Saratoga by the famous Saratoga, Mt. McGregor and Lake George Railroad. Situated 10½ miles north of Saratoga and elevated 1,000 feet above it. The Saratoga station is north of and adjoining the Waverly Hotel on North Broadway. From this point the track runs parallel with the Delaware and the Hudson Canal Company's Railway, and passes the Star, Empire, Red and "A" Springs on the right.

Near the water works, the road branches off to the left skirting along Loughberry Lake, leaving Excelsior Spring and Park on the right and pass-

ing Glen Mitchell on the left. From this point
the road is nearly straight for six miles and almost on a level grade. Wilton village lies at the
foot of Mt. McGregor, and it is from this point
that the ascent of the mountain proper begins.
The road winds around the mountain some four
miles, in the form of a huge letter S, with a uni-
form grade of 212 feet per mile. This railway
is essentially a pleasure road, trains will be
run to accommodate the public at all reasonable
hours, and affording plenty of time to examine
the many points of interest about this new and
popular resort, not the least of which is the
superb panorama presented from the Eastern
Outlook, embracing the whole northeastern part
of the State, the Green Mountains of Vermont,
and in the extreme distance the White Mountains
of New Hamshire.

LAKE GEORGE.—This famous resort. is easily
reached from Saratoga by the Delaware & Hudson
Canal Co. Trains leave for Caldwell, Fort William Henry Hotel) at 8.15 a. m., 10.00 a. m. 3.05
p. m. and 6.35 p. m. Caldwell is the metropolis
of Lake George and the county seat of Warren
County. The village contains besides the county
buildings, several well kept stores, three churches
and about 500 inhabitants. Here are the ruins
of Fort William Henry, the ruins of Fort George,
and about a mile distant, the remains of Fort

Hotel Balmoral

MT. McGREGOR, N.Y.

Gage, while the whole section is rich in historic associations, pleasant drives, delightful rambles and scenery of surprising beauty.

FORT WILLIAM HENRY HOTEL.—The fairest scenes are apt to lose their charm when viewed through an atmosphere of physical discomfort or amidst uncongenial company. Fortunately for the traveler, in 1868, (more than two centuries after the good old Father Jogues,) T. Roessle & Son may be said to have discovered "the Holy Lake." The old Wigwam at its head (southern end) they raised, enlarged and embellished, until it stood forth almost an Aladdin's palace, four to six stories in height, with Mansard roof, and a lake front of 334 feet. Along this entire front runs the great Piazza, which has become famous though the praise of the many habitues of Lake George.

It is twenty-four feet in width, and supported by a row of Corinthian columns thirty feet tall. The outlook from it at all times is little less than enchanting, commanding as it does the level reaches of the lake for miles, with a number of the most picturesque islands and promontories. In the evening, by full moonlight, or on a peaceful Sunday, while the orchestra discourses sacred music, and the only undertone is the flutter of cool dresses, dainty ribands and fans, and the low

FORT WILLIAM HENRY HOTEL.

voices of friendly promenaders, life here seems entirely worth living.

Under the dome (from the upper part of which a grand view of the Lake is obtained) is the general office, bazaar, book and cigar stand, etc. West of this is the drawing room, and on the east, suites of apartments, bijou parlors, and the large billiard hall, while at the back is the great dining hall, with accommodations for nearly 1000 guests. The lake and mountain air always circulating, supplies the best condiment. Fruits and vegetables are brought crisp and fresh daily from the Roessle farm near Albany, and the choicest meats and provisions from the metropolis.

Shooting galleries, croquet grounds, bowling alleys, etc. are to be found in the grove near the hotel.

A cabinet of Indian and historical curiosities, gathered from the locality, attracts great interest.

The hotel is elegantly furnished throughout, has a fast running elevator, and is lighted by gas and electricity. It is supplied with pure water from a mountain spring.

The crusine is identical in every way with that of "The Arlington, Washington." The same Chef' and assistants. The same Steward. The same Head Waiter with his excellent and full corps of carefully trained and experienced waiters. This being the only hotel on the entire Lake that does not rely for its table service on female help.

In the main office is the only General Ticket Office at Lake George, where baggage may be checked, and information obtained in regard to all distances. Stock reports are received hourly.

The lake steamboats land at the hotel dock, which is the headquarters for all the passenger, pleasure or excursion boats on the lake. A large number of steam and sailing yachts, and a flotilla of smaller boats are provided for the use of guests.

The livery stables attached keep constantly on hand saddle horses, buggies, buck-boards, phæ·tons and other carriages of all descriptions, to be had by applying at the office.

The lake steamboats *Horicon* and *Ticonderoga*, arrive morning and evening, bringing passengers from Lake Champlain and Whitehall, direct to the wharf of the Fort William Henry Hotel, where courteous attendants will always be in readiness to assist and serve the guests of this house.

The morning boat, *Horicon*, going northward through Lake George, connects at Baldwin with train for Ticonderoga, where connections are made with the Lake Champlain steamboats for the north, and trains southward for Saratoga, Schenectady, Troy and Albany. Coming south, she connects with cars at the Fort William Henry Hotel, for all points east, west and south.

The steamer *Ticonderoga*, and the pleasnre steamer *Lillie M. Price* leave the hotel daily, making excursions down the lake.

The orchestra, besides afternoon and evening concerts, plays in the Pagoda on the arrival of the boats, and the Old Gun at the battery of Fort William Henry booms forth hearty welcome.

THE ADIRONDACK RAILROAD.—Is very fruitful as an excursion route. scarcely a station on this road but what is worthy a stop-over to visit some delightful spot in the near vicinity. This line was commenced in 1865, and its entire length is 60 miles. Beginning at Saratoga Springs, where it makes a connection with the D. & H. C. Co., it runs in a northerly direction to North Creek, a distance of 58 miles, where connection is made by stage for the whole hunting and fishing grounds of the Adirondack wilderness. The wide, far-reaching landscape beheld as the train climbs up away from the village of springs ; the fertile farm lands of Greenfield, through which we pass ; the lovely glimpses of the Hudson in southern Hadley ; the picturesque crossing of the Sacondaga ; the mountain-walled valley, narrowing as we go still farther, at times creeping along close by the river-side, at others rising high above the foaming torrent, are beautiful pictures in the changing panorama, which combine to make this an exceedingly delightful ride.

A new stage line connects at North Creek for Blue Mountain Lake, a distance by road of 30 miles. During the summer season, a through sleeping coach will leave New York at 6.30 p. m. over the N. Y. C. & H. R. R. R., arriving at North Creek the following morning without change.

The trains of the Adirondack Company leave Saratoga on the arrival of the trains from south and north, from 10 to 10.30 A. M., and return in time to make connection with similar trains in the evening.

JESSUPS' LANDING—is seventeen miles from Saratoga, at the edge of the wild and mountainous Adirondack region. Objects of interest—the 70 feet falls in the Hudson, with the half-mile rapids above.

HADLEY—is reached twenty-two miles from Saratoga. This is situated at the confluence of the Hudson and Sacondaga Rivers. In a space of six miles the last-named stream has a fall of one hundred and sixty-four feet. This is also the station for Luzerne. The beauty of the natural scenery, and the salubrious climate yearly attract great numbers of visitors. There is a charm in its seclusion and serenity that cannot fail to win the sincere approbation of the tourist. During July and August a train will leave Saratoga about

9.20 p. m., on arrival of special leaving New York
at 4 p. m. for Hadley, arriving at 10.22 p. m.

RIVERSIDE.—Fifty miles from Saratoga, at this
station, we leave the cars for Chester, Pottersville,
Johnsburg, and Schroon Lake. A line of stages
run to Pottersville, distant six miles, thence to
the lake, one mile, where the small steamer
" Effingham" will take passengers up Schroon
Lake, to the Wells House, Mill Brook, and to
Schroon Village, nine miles distant.

NORTH CREEK is the present terminus of the
road, fifty-eight miles from Saratoga. A fine
bridge spans the river, and a new line of
stages start from here for Minerva, the Adirondack Iron Works, and Long Lake.

The Delaware and Hudson Canal Company run
ordinary and special trains to suit the convenience of visitors to many points of interests, one
of the most prominent is that of

LAKE GEORGE.—Take the train to Whitehall.
Ticonderoga, and Baldwin's; thence by steamer
on Lake George to Fort William Henry Hotel;
thence by railroad to Glenn's Falls and Fort Edward; back to Saratoga same day. This is the
most delightful excursion that can be completed
in one day from Saratoga. Should the party feel
inclined to make it two days, then take the morning train to Fort Edward, Glen's Falls; thence by
rail through wild and mountainous scenery to

Lake George. Besides, Lake George *must* be seen, even at a sacrifice of convenience, being as it is, the most charming place of its kind·· in America, if indeed it is to be surpassed anywhere in the wide world. The distance from the springs to the lake is about thirty miles.

Fare from Saratoga, through Lake George and return to Saratoga, tickets good for one day, $3.50.

The Boston, Hoosac Tunnel and Western Railway, having acquired the Saratoga Lake Railway, is very prolific in excursions. The first in order is one to

Saratoga Lake—One of the most delightful and enjoyable excursions from the springs, to the many beautiful resorts immediately surrounding the village, is to be made by the B. H. T. & W. Railway, to the lake, and thence by steamer to White Sulphur Springs. Their handsome new depot and waiting rooms are located at the junction of Lake avenue and Henry street. The cars make close connection at the lake with the company's beautiful and substantial little steamer Lady of the Lake. The best view of Lake Saratoga is from the top of Caldwell's Hill on the eastern bank. There the scene which meets the eye is calm and beautiful.

And now for the most enjoyable part of our trip—i. e. if any one portion can be said to be more enjoyable than another—we mean the sail around the lake on the company's steamer, Lady of the Lake. Starting out from the landing, the first prominent object of interest that strikes the view of the delighted excursionist is Snake Hill, a high, cone-shaped promontory, famous, it is

said, for the enormous numbers of snakes, which
make it their home, but as the company have engaged a special "St. Patrick" who has forbidden
them to enter the company's ground, no one need
be ,alarmed at their close proximity.. A half
hour's sail brings us to the White Sulphur Springs.

The White Sulphur Springs Hotel is elegantly
fitted up, and has several private dining rooms for
parties who desire to dine by themselves, and
ample accommodations for regular guests.

The grounds about the Hotel comprise over 100
acres of beautiful lawn, shaded by grand old
forest trees among which are miles of walks with
many charming retreats.

Several pretty cottages are on the grounds and
more are to be constructed. These are to be
rented to persons either with or without board at
the hotel. Elegant and commodious Bath Houses,
offering superior facilities for Sulphur and Mineral Baths, both hot and cold, are connected with
the Hotel. For further particulars address Mr.
T. C. Luther, proprietor.

SARATOGA BATTLE GROUNDS—.A visit to the
scene of the great battle of Saratoga, which ended
in the surrender of the British army under General Burgoyne to the Americans under Gates, will
occupy a pleasant, though a somewhat long day's
excursion. Take train on B. H. T. & W. Railway to Stillwater and drive to Bemis Heights,
dine at Schuylerville, and return same day or
next.

SARATOGA MONUMENT.—This fine monument
to commemorate the surrender of General Burgoyne is at Schuylerville, and well worth a visit.
The monument is now completed and President
Cleveland is expected to be present at its dedica-
tion in October next. Meantime it is open for
inspection, and special trains will be run every
day during the season by B. H. T. & W. Ry.
leave Saratoga about 9 a. m., returning about noon
giving ample time for visiting the monument.

There are many other excursions of shorter
length, which we have described under the head
of "Drives." The longer ones are limitless. in
number and extent. Our object is to suggest
those which naturally belong to Saratoga.

CHAPTER XIII.

AMUSEMENTS.

The question of providing amusement for the
vast number of visitors to Saratoga is in the ag-
gregate something appalling, but individually it
sinks into insignificance, for the visitors are, as a
class, willing to be pleased, and that is half the
battle. For a little amusement on the quiet go in
the morning to one of the principal springs and

MUSIC PAVILION IN CONGRESS SPRING PARK, SARATOGA.

watch the faces of the drinkers and you will ad.
mit it is a scene worthy the pencil of a "Ho-
garth." Of course it is the proper thing for every
one who goes to Saratoga to be ailing in some
particular, hence as soon as he rises in the morning his first thought is of the springs. Not having consulted a doctor, he pours his complaint
into the ear of some willing listener, and receives
gratuitous advice in plenty. To hear these inno-
cent mortals tell of their unruly stomachs (as
though any one cared for that portion of their
anatomy), and their blissful enthusiasm concerning their miraculous cures, is one of the amusements of Saratoga. In for a good time the visitor
hies for the spring, and in a glorious frame of
mind turns to see others drink. Their ways are
various, some imbibe vast glassfuls with a heroic
smile, as much as to say I told you I would do it,
some wrap their handkerchief round the glass for
fear of soiling their white gloves, and sip, sip,
trying all the time to make believe they like it,
which isn't true, others simply drink, and drink,
and drink, till the spectator is lost in wonder,
love and praise, to think they do not explode like
a defective soda-fountain. Some call it delicious ;
others, horrid ; and some don't drink at all. No
place in the world will so bring out the likes and
dislikes, weaknesses and small vanities of people,
as a Saratoga spring early in the morning. To

stand on one side and see the performance, serves as an exhilarant, and will make one good-natured for half a day.

INDIAN CAMP AND PARK (5–7 H, I).—In the grove on top of the hill, and at the corner of Congress, Circular and Spring streets, is a collection of promiscuous amusements for the children and somewhat frisky adult population. Archery, hobby-horse, whirligigs, bowling alley, shooting gallery, croquet lawn, photograph galleries, tenpins, ice cream, lemonade, &c., form some of the enticements of this fascinating play-ground.

INDIAN ENCAMPMENT.—This is somewhat different and ought not to be confounded with the Indian Camp and Park. This encampment is a few steps from Broadway, on Ballston Avenue, and is passed by all visitors going to Geyser and Vichy Springs. Here are to be found the general accompaniments of a gipsy life, also archery, rifle range, bowling alley, croquet ground, base-ball, bazar of curiosities, and the Circular Railway. A new attraction this year is a Gravity Railroad, on the Switchback principle; this road is 400 feet long.

CONGRESS SPRING PARK, (4, 5, 6, G, H, I).—Congress Park is located in the heart of the village, with its immediate neighborhood fronting the Grand Union, Congress Hall, Columbian, Clarendon and Windsor Hotels. The Columbian and

Congress Springs are within its grounds. The
park is laid out in a highly artistic manner. It
has a small lake in the centre, and its trees afford
the visitor a pleasant and shady retreat. Doring's
band gives concerts in this park three times a
day—diversified by occasional vocal concerts, bal-
loon ascents, and twice a week a grand display of
fireworks.

SARATOGA MUSEUM. —The building lately occupied by the Seltzer Spring Co., is now utilized for
the purpose of a museum by the Saratoga County
Cabinet, in the lower rooms there is a fine zoologi-
cal collection, and the upper rooms are devoted to
rare specimens in geology, mineralogy and arch-
æology.

THE SARATOGA HOP.—Music and dancing are
of course very important items in the catalogue
of Saratoga amusements. and the appointments
at Saratoga Springs, in this wise, are most ample
and excellent.   The guest dines and sups at ease
and leisure, and when the diurnal hour arrives for
the salutatory devotions of the evening, he or she
steals a glance at the approving mirror, calls the
conquering smile to the lips, points the expectant
toe with required grace, and floats at once into
the elysian maze.

The "Hop," when it reaches the proportions
and dignity of a ball, is an occasional and more
elaborate mystery, and is held at one particular

"house," in behalf of the whole; the toilet becomes a matter of life and death, and to the utter forgetfulness of the price of gold. The order of the dancing and the programme of the orchestra are solemnly considered and formally announced ; and last, though not least, agreeable refreshments are provided for the sustenance of the exhausted devotees.

It is not, however, on occasions only, frequent as they may be, that Saratoga dances. On the contrary, it is forever dancing or drinking—the one exercise being the omega as the other is the alpha of its butterfly life. Each and every night bands of skilled musicians discourse at the hotels, and those who will may waltz and polk unceasingly.

TRAVELLING AMUSEMENTS.–Saratoga is scarcely ever without some special attraction. Either an Opera diva, a comedy or dramatic company, a concert party, a circus, a menagerie, or some specialty, all of which pick up the dollars and depart, others taking their places, and so it goes on until the season wanes.

This season is promised a short season of English Opera by Her Majesty's Opera Co.

GARDEN PARTIES are now a feature in hotel life, and scarcely a week passes but there is one at some of the large hotels; these are nights of enchantment, and would required an Alladin to picture them in all their oriental splendor.

BOAT-RACES, BASE-BALL MATCHES, ETC. — Rowing Regattas are held at Saratoga Lake, and embrace races between college crews and other amateurs as well as professional oarsmen. These usually begin in July, and occur at intervals during the season.

Base-ball matches will be a new feature in Saratoga's amusements. A large plot of ground 600 feet square, has been enclosed and prepared for this purpose, with grand stand, refreshments, &c. This ground is on South Broadway, opposite the Cemetery. Matches with good clubs, races and other sports will take place nearly every afternoon.

THE SARATOGA RACES. — The famous race-course, which lies about a mile out of town, and which was surveyed and laid out in 1863 by Charles H. Ballard, is the largest in the Union, not even excepting the great Fashion Course, on Long Island, and the more modern Jerome Park in New York. It is a favorite resort of the leading "horsemen" of the land, and the best blooded steeds are brought hither every season for the display of their prowess in wind and limb. This year the meeting will be an exceptionally good one, every horse of known repute having been entered; nor is it to be wondered at, for the amount of money offered by the association for the regular racing days is from $80,000 to $100,000. There

will be two meetings, the first commencing July
24th and ending August 10th; the second commencing, August 12th, and ending August
28th. The regular racing days are Tues-
days, Thursdays, and Saturdays; but the
practice has been in former years, and will be
carried out this, to have extra races on the off
days, so that practically there will be races every
week day from July 24th to August 28th. From
the character and number of horses entered Mr.
Wheatey anticipates that this season will eclipse
everything in racing annals that ever took place
in America.

SARATOGA CLUB HOUSE.—This building is on
East Congress street, and opposite Congress Park.
It was formerly occupied by the late John Mor-
rissey. It is a fine building, beautifully surrounded and elegantly furnished. Here gentlemen will find a menu equal to many of the best
hotels, while there is all the freedom of a club-
house.

CHAPTER XIV.

PARKS.

CONGRESS SPRING PARK.—This fine park com-
prises almost the entire plot of ground encom-
passed by Broadway, Congress and Circular
streets. Originally a forest, possessing many
natural attractions, it has been materially improved by grading, draining, and the addition of
many architectural adornments, until it now pre-

sents a most beautiful appearance, and is one of
Saratoga's principal charms. During the year
1876, the Congress and Empire Spring Company
expended nearly $100,000 on these improvements,
and now it surpasses all other parks of equal size
in the United States in the beauty of its graceful
and artistic architecture. The grade of the low
ground was raised from two to seven feet, and a
new plan of drainage adopted, which involved in
its system the elegant new reservoir and the
charming miniature lake. The grand entrance is
at the junction of Congress street and Broadway,
near the Grand Union Hotel and Congress Hall,
on what is now called Monument Square. On
entering, turn to the right, and you may pass
through a short Colonnade to the graceful spring
house over the Columbian Spring, or from the entrance turn to the left through a longer colonnade,
and you come to the interior of the artistic pavilion over Congress Spring. In this interior the
Congress Spring water is passed by uniformed attendants, and you may partake of it while seated at
a little table upon which the water is served.
The process of drawing the water is novel, and
you will be interested to observe it, while the
mode of serving affords opportunity to drink at
leisure and at ease, without the jostling and spill-
ing incident to the old systems pursued at the
other springs in town. Passing down a few steps

DEER LODGE IN CONGRESS SPRING PARK,
SARATOGA SPRINGS, N. Y.

and along the colonnade, you reach the elegant *cafe*, where hot coffee and other refreshments may be partaken of while listening to the park music and enjoying the charming view of the lakes and grounds from the *cafe* pavilion. Passing from the *cafe*, you may stroll at will, visiting the lakes and the shaded lawns, and listening to the delightful music of the very celebrated Park Band, which plays morning, afternoon and evening. In the evening the band occupies the very unique and artistic music pavilion in the centre of the lake. Strolling along to the south part of the grounds you may visit the deer shelter and park, where are several animals that roam and skip about within the enclosure, greatly to the delight of the children and the amusement of the adults. In the park, amid the flowers and shrubs, strolling over the grass-coverd, shaded lawns, or lounging under the grand old forest trees, enchanted by the charming music—here it is that one may enjoy the supreme delights of a genuine rural summer resort. Every convenience for park enjoyment is here afforded, including abundant settees, and shade, and the security of efficient police supervision. The grounds are thoroughly lighted at night by the Weston Electric Light, rendering them available as a place of evening resort. The scene in the evening, on the occasion of one of the grand concerts, is remarkably brilliant and charmingly fascinating.

Admission to the park is regulated by tickets, for which a nominal charge is made. Single admission tickets, admitting to all except evening concerts, 10 cents each, or 25 tickets for $2, fifty for $3.50, one hundred for $6. No charge for children under ten years of age accompanied by older persons. Admission to grand and sacred evening concert, 25 cents, unless advertised otherwise. Tickets may be obtained at the entrance to the park.

Some may wonder that in a resort like Saratogo there is no park open to the public without charge, but such is the fact. Congress Park, however, supplies for this trifling charge the desirable seclusion and security of a private park.

Excelsior Park.—This park, on Spring Avenue, contains one hundred and eighty acres of land, extending from Lake Avenue to Loughberry Lake, and including the grove. A road leads north, around Excelsior Lake, to the Lough-berry Water Works, where the great Holly Engines continually pump the lake-water through the village. A few moments may be well spent here examining these splendid engines in motion.

Geyser Park.—This park embraces a tract of about 100 acres surrounding the Geyser Spring, and is open to visitors who are invited by numerous rustic chairs and settees, to enjoy the natural beauties of this charming vicinity. Leaving South

Broadway and going by Ballston Avenue we reach this park immediately after crossing the railway, from thence down to the spring, leaving the spring-house by the rear door, we enter upon the ramble and follow the shady path down into the dell. From the rustic bridge is a pretty view of the waterfall near the spring-house, and in the vicinity are several springs of varied mineral properties, more or less undeveloped, but indicating the great richness of this region in mineral waters.

Interlaken Park. — Saratoga Lake, the late residence of Frank Leslie, Publisher, Mr. Truax proprietor. Open to the public, free.

Woodlawn Park, belonging to Judge Henry Hilton, though private property, promises, through the owner's liberality, to be an Acadia, free to all visitors to Saratoga. It is located about a mile northwest of the village. About three hundred acres of wood, field and dell, which by the aid of hundreds of laborers and unlimited expenditure of money, has been turned into a magnificent park.

Yaddo. — The country seat of Mr. Spencer Trask, of New York, is on the road from Saratoga to the Lake. It contains about 160 acres, and is a charming spot. Mr. Trask has decided to allow parties driving to the lake, the opportunity of going through his grounds, which they may do either in going or returning.

CHAPTER XV.

COMMERCIAL FEATURES.

The all absorbing feature of business in Saratoga is how to entertain its visitors, and very nearly the whole population is engaged in this business, either directly or indirectly, and be the season good, or only moderate, they are all benefited to a greater or less extent. True, the bottling and selling of its mineral waters is a commercial feature of no small limit. Some of the springs are very valuable, and their waters held in general esteem, hence their facilities for bottling and shipping are quite on an extensive scale, the amount of capital invested varying from a few hundreds to one million dollars.

The hotel interest is something fabulous, the amount of capital invested in this business can only be counted by millions, and in Saratoga are to be found some of the finest hotels on the face of the globe, their accommodations varying from 10 to 2,000 persons. No one who has been in Saratoga during the months of July or August, and seen the trains unloading their hundreds of visitors, and the hotel omnibuses continually rattling on the pavement with their loads of human freight, but must have been impressed with the magnitude of the hotel business. The Boarding House business, both public and private, is quite a commercial feature, and a great many of the more respected citizens are engaged in it ; probably all told the boarding houses can and do accom-modate as many guests as the hotels.

The number of boarding houses probably reaches one hundred and fifty, and their accommodation varies from the modest half dozen to the pretentious 200. Hence it will be seen that in the boarding house business there is a vast amount of capital invested.

Saratoga, however, is not lacking in other business interests ; its livery business is a large one ; its news rooms and book stores are equal to many city establishments. Photography is also a special feature, and amongst the best in this line may be mentioned Mr. W. H. Baker, of 448 Broadway, and Mr. E. A. Record at the corner Broadway and Phila streets, at either establishment first class work may be relied upon. Mr. H. Voullieme, of 361 Broadway, is the leading man in choice confections and ice cream, also in rare and beautiful stones.

Mr. Tracy A. Record, of No. 334 Broadway, will supply the visitor with everything in the way of fancy goods, delicate carvings, Saratoga views, dolls, curiosities and notions generally. Saratoga has many good stores, and probably very **few** towns of its size can boast of as much plate glass.

The Drug Store of Mr. T. H. S. Pennington, at 400 Broadway, is quite a noted place in Saratoga, and here will be found everything both useful and ornamental usually kept in the best drug stores of our large cities.   Mr. Pennington is the Pharmacist to the United States Hotel, he is also sole proprietor and manufacturer of Pennington's Norwegian Troches, a most valuable remedy for diseases peculiar to the bronchial passages. These Troches are highly recommended by eminent men, as especially applicable for public speakers and vocalists.   Mr. Pennington is highly - respected in Saratoga, yet it has not been without a struggle that he has obtained that position.

In 1867 he entered the service of F. T. Hill & Co., Saratoga, as summer clerk, and eventually became the manager of the business under this firm.   When the firm of F. T. Hill & Co. was succeeded by F. A. White and B. Schermerhorn, Mr. Pennington, whose ability was appreciated by these gentlemen, was continued as manager of the establishment, and in the year 1880 he bought out the interest of his employers, and became the absolute proprietor.   Since that time the pharmacy has increased yearly in popularity, and to-day there is not an establishment of its kind in Saratoga that enjoys more of the confidence of the public than this house.

Mr. Pennington is a member of the American
Pharmaceutical Association, and his ability as a
pharmacist is recognized not only by the home
public, but also by the large summer population
that annually make Saratoga its home.

The Book Store of Mr. E. R. Stevens is at the
corner of Broadway and Spring street, facing
Congress Hall and the Grand Union Hotels. Here
will be found guide books including Lee's Guide
to Saratoga, souvenir albums, also a beautiful
stock of Japanese Articles, and in French China
and Colored Glass lettered "Saratoga" suitable
for souvenirs. Mr. Stevens also keeps a large
stock of Fine Stationery, Pocket Books, Knives,
Card Cases, Albums, Gold Pens etc., also Lawn
Tennis, Croquet and games of all kinds; another
feature of this store is its 800 volume circulating
library of the most valuable and popular works
of the day.

At No. 460 Broadway, is the original New York
Store, "open the year round." Here you will find
novelties in millinery, laces, fancy goods, hosiery,
switches, braids, jewelry, gents' furnishing goods,
etc. Mr. Rix is well known for his fair dealing,
not only to "Saratogians," but to all visitors.
He employs only the best milliners and sales-ladies
and in prices will compete with any New York
house. The quality and style of his stock is excellent, and the variety is fully equal to the de-
mands of the summer trade at this fashionable
watering-place.

AFTERNOON IN CONGRESS SPRING PARK,
SARATOGA SPRINGS, N. Y.

CHAPTER XVI.

CHURCHES.

Saratoga Springs is well supplied with church accommodation. A stranger entering almost any of the churches during the fall, winter or spring, would be apt to arrive at the conclusion that the people of Saratoga were not a church-going class. But it must be chronicled that the churches are designed for the accommodation of both transient and permanent residents, and that the former, during the summer-months, out-number the latter, probably at any time by two to one. The churches taken generally are both commodious and elegant. The regular pastors are men of marked ability, but during the season the pulpits are more often occupied by eminent divines from various parts of the Union, some having quite a national reputation.

The Episcopal church is on Washington street.
The Methodist church is on Washington street.
The Presbyterian church is on Broadway.
The Baptist church is on Washington street.
The Congregational church is on Caroline street
The Catholic church is on South Broadway.
The Second Presbyterian church is on Spring st.
The Free Methodist chapel is on Regent street.
The hours of service and names of the pastors may be found in the Saturday edition of the Saratoga daily papers.

CHAPTER XVII.

NEWSPAPERS.

Daily and Weekly Saratogian.—B. F. Judson, Publisher. Summer Season $2. Office, 8 Arcade.

Saratoga Daily Register.—Published during the summer season. J. C. Cowdery, Publisher. Office, 10 Lake Avenue.

Saratoga Journal, Daily and Weekly.—Price, Daily, $6; Weekly, $1.50 a year. David F. Ritchie, Editor. Office, Phila street.

Saratoga Sun.— Published every Saturday. Price, $1.25 a year. E. P. Howe, Publisher. Office, Town Hall.

Saratoga Eagle.— Published every Friday. Price, $1 a year. John Johnson & Co., 10 Lake Avenue.

CHAPTER XVIII.

PUBLIC INSTfTUTIONS.

Saratoga is well prepaied to accommodate her guests in regard to public institutions and enterprises.

Town Hall (101–9-10 F).—This building is on Broadway, at the corner of Lake avenue, and is used mainly for the offices of the village authorities, and during the summer season by the Court of Appeals. The large room on the second floor is utilized for public meetings, conventions, concerts and theatricals.

Board of Education.—This Board has its offices in the Town Hall.

Surrogate's Court.—A Court is held in the Town Hall every alternate Monday.

Post Office (90–7 F).—The post office is in the Arcade, on the east side of Broadway, between the Grand Union and the United States Hotels, on the opposite side.

Railroad Depot (91-6, 7, D).—The railway depot of the D. & H. C. Co. is located one block west of Broadway, on Division street.

Express Office (92–7 D).—The express office is annexed to the depot.

Railroad Depot.—The Depot of the B. H. T. & W. Railway is on Lake Avenue, corner of Henry Street.

Congress Spring Park (85–3, 4, 5, 6, G, H I).— Congress Spring Park is located in the heart of the village, with its immediate neighborhood fronting the Grand Union, Congress Hall, Columbian, Clarendon and Windsor Hotels.

Temple Grove Ladies' Seminary.—This Institution is beautifully situated in a grove in the eastern part of the village, on what was formerly called Temple Hill, hence the name. The grounds occupy the whole square on Spring Street, between Circular and Regent streets.

Child's Convalescent Home.—Is located on Ballston avenue.

Saratoga Humane Society.—Room 20, Ainsworth Place. Organized 1879. Number of members, 125. Office hours, 12 to 1 and 5 to 6 P. M. Meetings held the last Wednesday of each month.

Saratoga Athenæum.—This Institution is in Exchange Place, corner of Caroline street and Broadway. It is well supplied with books, papers and periodicals.

DR. DOWNES'

DENTAL PARLORS,

14 Barclay Street,

NEW YORK.

Three doors from Astor House.

One door from St. Peter's Church.

We are only five minutes from the Liberty, Cortlandt, Barclay and Chambers Street Ferries.

THE

Saratoga Daily Register

Published Daily During the Summer Season.

Is published solely for the visitors to Saratoga, and contains all the news concerning Arrivals, Society, Races, Hops, and the Programmes of the Concerts given daily on the hotel piazzas.

Is the most Popular Paper, and has more Circulation than any paper published in Saratoga.

IS THEREFORE THE BEST ADVERTISING MEDIUM!

CHAPTER XIX.

BATTLE OF SARATOGA

This battle was fought and won upon the elevated lands at Bemis Heights, two and a half miles from the Hudson, in the town of Stillwater. The visitor may obtain all desired information respecting the precise localities of the struggle from residents and cicerones on the grounds. At the time of the eventful Battle of Saratoga the American troops were in high feather at their successes in the defeat of St. Leger and at Stark's brilliant performance at Bennington, which had occurred during the latter part of the preceding month. The enemy's forces in the neighborhood were believed to be in a bad way generally, and all parties were ignorant of the British progress on the Hudson below and further south. Troops poured in from all quarters, and General Gates was in good trim for the work that soon fell to him.

As an illustration as to how chance seems to rule in war, there is recorded a story, which, with a different sequel, might have entirely altered the relative fortunes of Burgoyne and Gates at that time. Clinton, the English commander on the Hudson, had dispatched a messenger to Burgoyne, announcing his success and promising him relief; which message, had it but safely reached its destination, might have led to an avoidance of the fatal rencontre into which the English General was led at Saratoga. The message contained the brief words, "*nous y voici*, and nothing between us but Gates." It was enclosed in a silver bullet.

The messenger fell in with a squad of American troops, whom he unluckily mistook for friends, as they chanced just then to be arrayed in red coats, recently captured from an English store-ship. He incautiously divulged his errand, when he discovered his sad mistake, and Burgoyne lost his message.

The Americans were entrenched on a spur of hills approaching the Hudson. Earthworks were thrown across the meadow to the river. The heights were to the north and west. Breastworks were projected in a semi-circle nearly a mile to the north and redoubts established at intervals September 19th Burgoyne's army advanced. The left was commanded by Riedesel along the river. Frazer's division took the west and right, and Burgoyne led the centre, his object being a union with Frazer's division in the rear of the American camp. The Americans charged the enemy with great impetuosity. The battle was fiercely con. tested. The Americans often scattering before the British bayonets, and the British frequently

fleeing from the Americans' deadly fire. At
night the Americans retired into their camp. The
British held the field with a barren victory. They
were foiled in their main object, but convinced
that those who fight for freedom and for country
fight for victory or death.

Calm after storm followed ; and the two armies,
skilfully entrenched, lay face to face from Sept.
20th to Oct. 7th—the Americans exultant, the
British dejected. The former restful in their con-
scious strength ; the latter restless under impend-
ing disaster. The Americans had recaptured
Ticonderoga and the Lake George garrisons. No
aid came to Burgoyne from the Lower Hudson.
October 7th Burgoyne attacked the American
left with select troops, led in person by Riedesel,
Frazer and Phillips. The Americans rushed furi-
ously upon their adversaries, and so terrible was
the onslaught that in less than twenty minutes
"the flower of the army" was completely routed.
Burgoyne took command, and rushed into the
thickest of the battle to rally his army ; but he
could not check a hurricane. The Americans
swept on, like a resistless storm, and drove their
enemies from the field. One of "the fifteen de-
cisive battles of history" had been fought and
American Independence assured.

Burgoyne's army took refuge under the redoubts during the 8th of October, and the day

was spent in skirmishing. At nine o'clock of that same night Burgoyne ordered a full retreat, and next day encamped his army on the heights above Schuylerville. He was followed by the Americans, surrounded and compelled to surrender. On the 17th of October, 1777, the British army marched out of their camps under their own officers and laid down their arms. General Burgoyne presenting his sword to General Gates, and as a plucky general should be he was received with all military honors.

BEMIS' HEIGHTS, the scene of this famous engagement between General Burgoyne and General Gates, is about 15 miles distant, in Stillwater, and is visited by large numbers of people. On the ground has been erected a monument to commemorate this great and closing battle for American Independence.

Tourists visiting New York will find the *Hotel Brunswick* at the corner of 26th Street and 5th Avenue a first class hotel in every respect. It is conducted on both American and European plans. Mitchell, Kinzler & Southgate, Proprietors.

THE THOUSAND ISLAND HOUSE, Alexandria Bay on the River St. Lawrence, is one of the finest summer resort hotels in the United States. It is in the very centre of the best fishing grounds, and is visited annually by many of the best families. For descriptive guide book and all particulars as to rates etc., address R. H. Southgate, President, or C. P. Clemes, Manager.

OCEAN HOUSE, NEWPORT, R. I.—Is at once the finest and largest house in Newport. It is the summer home of the most refined circles of American society. Fronting on Bellevue Avenue, the fashionable drive, and adjoining the famous Casino, it is the very centre of Newport life and society. The house is kept up to the highest standard of excellence. Messrs. J. G. Weaver & Sons, are the Proprietors.

When in Washington, D. C., be sure and stop at *Willard's Hotel* corner of 14th Street and Pennsylvania Avenue. The house is first class in every respect, it is near the White House and all the government offices, places of Amusement &c. Mr. O. G. Staples late of the Thousand Island House is the proprietor.

Tourists going to the Pacific Coast will find the *St. Louis and San Francisco Railway* the most agreeable route. It runs through a delightful section of country. The road is in first class condition, the coaches the finest that are made, while the fares are as low or lower than any other route. Write to Mr. D. Wishart, G. P. A., St. Louis, Mo., for particulars and pamphlets.

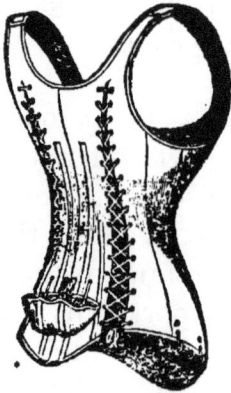

SARATOGA

STAR SPRING,

SARATOGA SPRINGS, N. Y.

SARATOGA STAR SPRING WATER

Sold on Draught and in Bottles.

In Cases, quarts...........................2 dozen.
In Cases, pints...........................4 dozen.

This Water contains 2 grains Iodine, and 14 grains
Bromide in each quart.

SOLD ON DRAUGHT AND IN BOTTLES.

By Dealers and Druggists throughout the United
States and Canadas.

Orders to Dealers or the Company promptly filled.

This is the only Spring in Saratoga that is tubed in
the rock, which is of itself sufficient recom-
mendation to warrant it as the purest
of mineral waters.

D. H. PORTER,   .   Proprietor.

**Contains More Iodine Than Any Known Spring,
Endorsed for 40 Years.**

THE

HATHORN SPRING WATER,

Is sold in glass bottles only—pints and quarts.

The annual sale in bottles of this most popular mineral water *very largely* exceeds the sale in bottles of all other natural bottled mineral waters of Saratoga combined.

One Case, 4 dozen pints,   -   -   - $6.50
One Case, 2 dozen quarts,   -   -   - $5.50

Delivered free on board at Saratoga or New York, securely packed for shipment. Free delivery in New York, Brooklyn or Jersey City. Discounts to the Trade,

SOLD BY GROCERS, WINE MERCHANTS, DRUGGISTS AND HOTELS,

The quart bottles have the name blown in the glass. "Hathorn Spring, Saratoga, N. Y.," and the pint is a plain bottle with printed label.

Orders by mail, addressed to the undersigned, for shipment to any point, will receive prompt attention, and will be forwarded to destination by the best freight lines.

E, H. HATHORN,

Hathorn Spring,   Saratoga, N. Y.

SARATOGA CHAMPION SPRING,

RICHEST IN MINERALS OF ALL SARATOGA WATERS.

THE BEST CATHARTIC

Possessing more Magnesia than any other spring at Saratoga.

BOTTLED EXACTLY AS IT FLOWS FROM THE SPRING, AND WITHOUT ANY ARTIFICIAL MANIPULATION WHATEVER.

Delivered to customers in New York or Brooklyn, at $6 per case, discount to the trade. Address all orders direct to the

SARATOGA CHAMPION SPRING,

Saratoga Springs, N. Y.

FRANKLIN HOUSE,

L. L. BRINTNALL, Prop.

CHURCH STREET, - First House from Broadway.

TERMS REASONABLE.

HOLDEN HOUSE,

MR. C. H. HOLDEN, Prop.

423 Broadway, Saratoga Springs, N. Y.

Third door North of U. S. Hotel.

TERMS REASONABLE.

HOWLAND HOUSE,

No, 573 Broadway, Saratoga Springs,

This house is located on the west side of Broadway, opposite the Waverley Hotel. Great additions and improvements have recently been added. Accommodations can be furnished for sixty persons. The broad piazzas, comfortable rooms, and first-class service, combine to make it a most desirable stopping place. Address,

J. HOWLAND,

Saratoga Springs, N, Y.

MANSION HOUSE,

EXCELSIOR PARK, SARATOGA SPRINGS.

Near Excelsior Spring, pure country air, grounds well shaded and all appointments first-class. Best accommodation for private carriages.

MARY E. SIMMONS, Proprietor.

NEW ENGLAND HOUSE,

125 Woodlawn Ave, (formerly Matilda St.,) *Saratoga Springs, N. Y.*

Dr. O. Ford, Eclectic Physician, Medical Electrician and Hydropathist. Three minutes' walk north of depot. Open the year round. Good homes for invalids and pleasure seekers. Baths, &c. Convenient to the Springs. Empire water fresh every morning. Prices reasonable.

P. H. ANSLOW, Manager.

PRIVATE BOARDING.

MRS. ROBERT GILLIS,

31 Caroline Street, Saratoga Springs, N. Y.

OPEN ALL YEAR. **TERMS REASONABLE.**

MRS. D. T. CARPENTER,

PRIVATE BOARDING,

55 Phila Street, Cor. Henry.

SARATOGA SPRINGS, N. Y

MRS. J. P. SCOVILL'S

FIRST-CLASS

PRIVATE BOARDING HOUSE,

57 Phila, cor. Henry Street, Saratoga Springs, **N. Y**

PRIVATE BOARDING,

MRS. M. A. MAGEE,

103 Circular Street, Corner of Phila.

P. O. BOX, 560. SARATOGA SPRINGS, N. Y.

TERMS MODERATE.

PRIVATE BOARDING

R. CHURCHILL,

No. 121 Lake Avenue, Corner Harrison Street.

Large and Beautiful Grounds with Shade Trees.

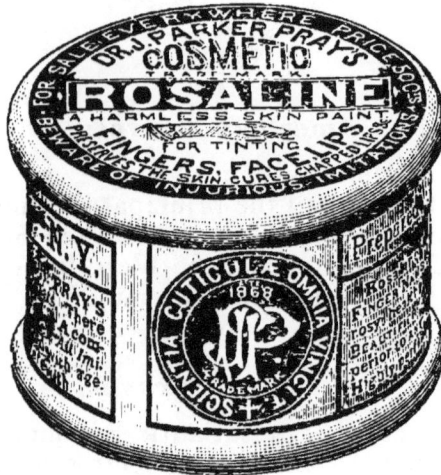

Fleischmann's

VIENNA MODEL BAKERY.

Ladies' and Gentlemen's Cafe and Restaurant.

Ask Your Grocers Throughout the State for Bread and Rolls from

✻FLEISCHMANN'S✻

Broadway and 10th St.,   NEW YORK.

Willard's Hotel,

Washington, D. C.

There is probably no hotel whose name is so familiar to the general public as Willard's hotel, Washington, D. C. The growth of this popular hostelry has kept pace with the increase and prosperity of the capital. Seventy-five years ago, soon after Washington was selected as the seat of Government, it had its beginning in the modest and unassuming City Hotel. On the same locality now stands the Willard's of to-day, with a frontage of 150 feet on Pennsylvania Avenue, and 350 feet on Fourteenth Street, with accommodations for a thousand guests. In the appointments of this palatial hotel, money, unstinted, has been expended, and every convenience that taste and experience can suggest has been provided for the comfort of the guests. Indeed, throughout all the house, the rooms are furnished with all the luxuries and comforts that wealth can supply even in the costliest private residences. There are but few hotels in the world so completely and expensively furnished as "Willards." The hotel has a world wide reputation for the excellence of its table, and Mr. O. G. Staples, the proprietor, is determined that all that money and skill can do, shall be done to maintain the standard and, if possible, to improve upon the past. Any of our readers who may visit Washington should be sure and stop at "Willard's."

Ocean House

NEWPORT, R. I.

FRONTING ON BELLEVUE AVE.,

THE GRAND DRIVE.

A REFINED SUMMER HOME FOR FAMILIES.

ADJOINING THE FAMOUS CASINO.

JOHN G. WEAVER & SON,

Proprietors.

CONGRESS SPRING

THE STANDARD MINERAL WATER

CATHARTIC, ALTERATIVE. A specific for disorders of the STOMACH, LIVER, and KIDNEYS, ECZEMA, MALARIA, and all impurities of the BLOOD.

SO enviable a name has this famous Mineral Water, that the man-agers of inferior mineral springs, desirous of imitating the natural purity of the bottled water of Congress Spring, inject a powerful acid in their bottled water to preserve the crude ingredients in solu-tion, – being so heavily laden with

LIME AND IRON DEPOSIT.

With such contrivances, bogus testimonials and doctored analysis cards they seek to rival the pure medicinal waters of Congress Spring.

THE regular season visitors to Saratoga fully understand these crude harsh waters, many of them after painful experiences. *In proof of this fact we can produce a great many responsible names.* but the Saratoga visitors without experience, and many who use the bottled waters (often labeled as curatives for disorders which they positively aggravate), should remember, that crude mineral waters produce headache, a sense of burning and internal irritation, and do irreparable injury to the digestive organs and kidneys.

CONGRESS WATER, PURE, NATURAL AND RELIABLE.

NONE GENUINE SOLD ON DRAUGHT.

For sale by Druggists, Grocers, Wine Merchants and Hotels.

Bottle (C) Mark.

LEWANDO'S

French Dyeing & Cleansing Establish't

Principal Offices :

**New York : Fifth Ave., cor. W. 14th St.
Boston, Mass., 17 Temple Place.**

BRANCH OFFICES:

NEW YORK CITY, 731 Sixth Ave., near 42d St.
276 Eighth Ave., opposite Grand Opera House.
PHILADELPHIA, Pa., 1409 Chestnut Street.
BALTIMORE, Md., 16 North Charles Street.
PROVIDENCE, R. I., 275 Westminster Street.
NEWPORT, R. I., 293 Thames Street.
BOSTON (Highlands), 2206 Washington Street.
BOSTON (South) 393 Broadway.
LYNN, Mass., 3 Market Street.
WATERTOWN, Mass., Galen Street.

WORKS: NEW YORK CITY AND WATERTOWN, MASS.
Price List Sent Free.

☞ *To obtain an* **Everlastingly** *" Beautiful Complexion and Elegant Contour of Form," see page 6*

www.ingramcontent.com/pod-product-compliance
Lightning Source LLC
Chambersburg PA
CBHW020858270326
41928CB00006B/761